RUPERT

OF THE

RHINE

RUPERT

OF THE

RHINE

�֍ ✖ ✖

Maurice Ashley

Hart Davis, MacGibbon London

Granada Publishing Limited
First published in Great Britain 1976 by Hart-Davis, MacGibbon Ltd
Frogmore, St Albans, Hertfordshire AL2 2NF and
3 Upper James Street, London W1R 4BP

ISBN 0 246 10793 6

Printed in Great Britain by
Butler & Tanner Ltd, Frome and London

CONTENTS

LIST OF MAPS

INTRODUCTION

High among those who were legends in their own lifetimes and have remained so ever since is Prince Rupert of the Rhine. This nephew of King Charles I was only twenty-three years old when he came to support his uncle's cause in the English Civil War, but he was already a veteran soldier with some nine years of military experience behind him. This, as much as his royal blood, singled him out for high rank, and Charles at once gave him the virtually independent command of the royalist cavalry.

Rupert's career as a cavalry leader lasted only four years, but his legend belongs entirely to that performance. His long apprenticeship is forgotten; the many years of his service at sea, first fighting *against* the British Navy during the Common-wealth, then, under Charles II, fighting *with* it against the Dutch, and finally succeeding his cousin the Duke of York (later James II) at the head of it, are quite overshadowed. Prince Rupert is remembered always in the company of leaders on horseback, men like Marshal Murat or General J. E. B. Stuart. He was a cavalryman *par excellence*.

Above all, this was an achievement of personality. This very young man at once became an outstanding figure in royalist circles – indeed, I dare say many people would be hard put to it to name another royalist commander. His good looks, his impetuous courage, his deliberately cultivated *panache* made him an exception – an inspirer of troops – but first they had to be made into troops. It was Rupert's less regarded sheer profes-sionalism that enabled him to turn the crowd of young aristo-crats, country gentry and grooms who followed the King's ban-ner into soldiers at all. His ability to do this, and to keep the King's cavalry a formidable force in the field to the end (so much so that to this day the royalists are often called 'the

Cavaliers'), provides the hard core of truth that has supported the legend for three centuries.

On the battlefield itself, Rupert's quality as a leader is less certain. His horsemen constantly asserted a superiority over their immediate opponents, but their endemic lack of discipline – a virtue almost impossible to inculcate in a force so recruited – invariably threw the advantage away. When Cromwell matched them with 'men of spirit' who were also disciplined and obedient to their orders, the royalist superiority perceptibly diminished, and when the whole parliamentary army began to take on similar qualities, the royal cause was lost. Unfortunately, the image of the headlong charge carried through without check planted itself in the minds of succeeding generations of British cavalry to their grave disadvantage and loss.

What we shall never know is what Rupert would or could have done with soldiers as professional as he was himself. What we do know is that in a very short space of time, and with most unpromising material, he was able to impose his personality and his will on friends and enemies alike, and it is the rare quality at the heart of this achievement that justifies his fame.

John Terraine

Chapter One

✲

MILITARY
APPRENTICESHIP

Rupert of the Rhine, wrote his contemporary, Sir Philip Warwick, was 'a brave prince and a hopeful soldier'; '*il estoit toujours
Soldat*', he added, by which he meant that Rupert was never
either a statesman or a politician. By study, practice and experience he trained himself to be a commander of men both on
land and sea, dedicating himself completely to the profession
he had chosen. Though he was not always victorious, he was
one of the outstanding generals in Europe during the seventeenth century.

Rupert was born in Prague, capital of Bohemia, on 17
December 1619. His mother was a daughter of King James I
of England and his father was Frederick V, the Elector Palatine,
one of the seven princes in Germany who were entitled to choose
the Holy Roman Emperor. One of Rupert's great-grandfathers
had been William the Silent, the hero of the Dutch war of independence against the Spaniards and the founder of the republic
of the United Netherlands. From him, it may be assumed,
Rupert inherited his martial ardour. The Prince Palatine and
'that lovely Princess, the Lady Elizabeth', as she was described
at the time, were married on St Valentine's Day, 14 February
1613, in Whitehall chapel, amid scenes of general rejoicing. But
the bride's happy smile on her wedding day was afterwards con-
strued by the superstitious as an example of hubris, forecasting
disaster. Five years later her husband by his actions was to strike
the spark that lit a war which was to devastate Europe for thirty
years.

The throne of Bohemia, as of Hungary, had traditionally
been a perquisite of the Holy Roman Emperor, who ruled
the widespread Habsburg lands from Vienna and was the

Seventeenth-century Prague: an engraving by Wenceslaus Hollar.

acknowledged leader of all the German princes. But a majority of the Bohemians were Protestants who resented the election in June 1617 of the Emperor Matthias's heir, Archduke Ferdinand of Styria, who was a devout Roman Catholic, brought up by Jesuits, as their king. Although before his coronation Archduke Ferdinand had guaranteed the 'Letter of Majesty' which bestowed liberty of conscience on all Bohemian Protestants, a row developed over the building of two Lutheran churches on royal estates and led directly to a coup d'état. In May 1618 two regents appointed in Vienna, who had been against the confirmation of the Letter of Majesty, were thrown by Protestant rebels out of the windows of the Hradschin palace in Prague (though by the intervention of the Virgin Mary, as it was maintained, they escaped with their lives); and after more than a year of complicated manoeuvring the Estates of Bohemia repudiated Ferdinand and offered the crown to Frederick V, the Elector Palatine, who was then twenty-two. In his capital of Heidelberg the young Elector hesitated, first because he was

2

aware of his constitutional duty to the Emperor and secondly because many of his advisers, including his father-in-law, James I of England, were against acceptance. But ambition to be a king triumphed over caution. In the first week of November 1619 he and his English wife were successively crowned in Prague Cathedral.

Six weeks later their son Rupert was born, the third of a family which was to total eight sons and five daughters. Rupert's earliest biographer was to write: 'the crowning of his mother while she bore him in her womb seemed not to be the presage of an ordinary fate.'

Hopeful of the support of all the Protestant princes, the King of Bohemia spent a year in a glow of optimism, visiting his new dominions and planning hunting parties for his wife. Elizabeth conceived another child, who was to be Rupert's favourite brother, Maurice. But the Archduke Ferdinand, who had been elected Emperor two days after Frederick had been chosen King of Bohemia, regarded him as a rebel and a usurper and

3

The 'defenestration' of two Roman Catholic Regents from the Hradschin palace at Prague on 23 May 1618. This incident was the opening shot in a Bohemian Protestant revolt which culminated in the coronation of Frederick V, Elector Palatine, as King of Bohemia.

resolved to overthrow him. On 8 November 1620 an imperial army decisively defeated the Bohemian troops and their Protestant allies at the Battle of White Hill, a broad eminence which dominated Prague. 'The Winter King and Queen', as they were henceforward called, fled their capital. In the general excitement their one-year-old child was almost forgotten. But a courtier found him and flung him into the boot of the last coach to leave Prague.

Queen Elizabeth was unable to return to Heidelberg, for the Lower Palatinate was already overrun by Spanish troops serving as allies of the Emperor. Instead she sought refuge with her brother-in-law, the pusillanimous Elector George of Brandenburg, who reluctantly allowed her to occupy the castle of Küstrin, where she gave birth to her fourth son. 'He will have to be a soldier,' she said; so she named him Maurice after the

Frederick V, Elector Palatine, the 'Winter King' of Bohemia, father of Prince Rupert.

eldest son of William the Silent, Prince Maurice Count of Nassau, one of the foremost commanders of his day. Elizabeth left Küstrin with her sons as soon as she could, to secure a far warmer welcome from her husband's uncles at The Hague. Prince Frederick Henry, who was to succeed his brother Maurice as Captain-General of the United Netherlands, gave up his own palace for her immediate use. The beautiful exiled queen never lacked friends and admirers. She settled down

5

Rupert's mother, Queen Elizabeth of Bohemia,
sister of King Charles I of England.

happily to the social amenities in Holland while her husband
was intriguing to regain his lost thrones, and sent Rupert to
be brought up and educated in Leyden, the foremost university
town in Europe.

It was rumoured that neither father nor mother was sufficiently devoted to their large brood of children. As early as
January 1620 the English gossip, John Chamberlain, had
written to a friend: 'No rejoicings, as usual, at the birth of the
Bohemian prince: the King is said to be a strange father who
will neither fight for his children nor pray for them.' Of the
Queen it was alleged that she did not exert herself unduly to
win her children's affections and was glad to pack her sons off
to Leyden. But it is known that Rupert was to become her
favourite, while her husband was proud of the precocious apti-
tudes exhibited by the child prince, writing of him when he
was but three: 'the little Rupert is very learned to understand
so many languages.'

In fact Rupert benefited greatly from his education. He was
soon able to speak High Dutch and Low Dutch fluently, though
his native language was German, and he read English, French,
Spanish, Italian and Latin – he never had the slightest difficulty
over languages. His mother was determined that he, as well
as Maurice, should become a soldier, so that he might espouse
the cause of his father and also of his father's uncles who were
still absorbed (after a truce that ended in 1619) in the long-
drawn-out war of independence against Spain. Prince Rupert
delighted in the exercise of horses, the use of arms, and the
study of the art of fortification. He was also so thoroughly
indoctrinated with the Calvinist faith that he was never
tempted to become a Roman Catholic. His father, who understandably suffered from melancholia, never recovered his
thrones, though his spirits were uplifted by the triumphs of King
Gustavus Adolphus of Sweden when he invaded Germany in
1630. But the death of this Protestant hero in his moment of
victory at the Battle of Lützen in November 1632 broke the
Elector Frederick's heart. Within a fortnight he was dead of
plague miles away from his family in Holland. In the very next
year Rupert gained his first experiences of war when he was
allowed to join his great-uncle Frederick Henry, now the Dutch
captain-general, at the siege of Rheinberg, which lay to the west

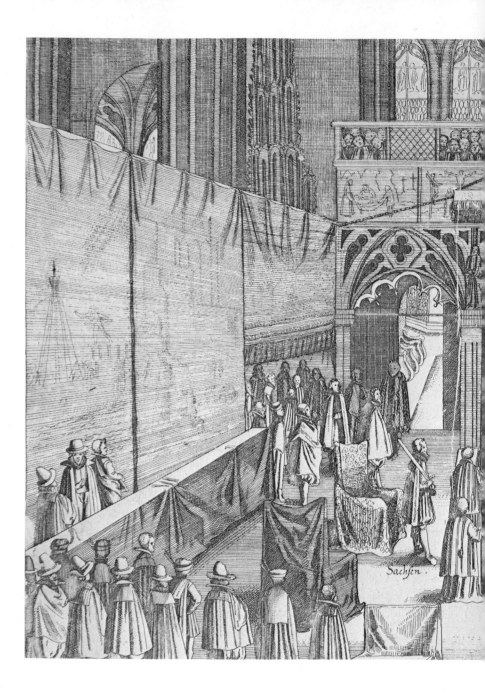

Sachsen.

Ferdinand II being crowned Holy Roman
Emperor on 9 September 1619.

of the Rhine some forty miles from the Dutch frontier. His mother had consented to her sons thus going to the wars. 'He cannot too soon be a soldier,' she said of Rupert, 'in these active times.' He was not yet fourteen. After the fall of Rheinberg, when the boy returned in triumph to his mother at The Hague, the ladies of the court vied with each other in their enthusiasm to welcome him back.

The University of Leyden seemed rather dull after all that; so two years later when he was over fifteen, as one of his biographers wrote, 'he made his first real campaign as a volunteer in the lifeguard of the Prince of Orange; rejecting all distinctions of his rank, discharging all the duties and sharing all the hardships of the private soldier.' In that year, 1635, the

France of Cardinal Richelieu had allied itself with the Dutch against the Spaniards, still struggling to regain control of the northern Netherlands in alliance with the Emperor Ferdinand II, who had deprived Rupert's father of his hereditary possessions. The fighting took place in Brabant, part of the southern Netherlands. The French and Dutch captured and sacked the town of Tirlemont, but afterwards they were unsuccessful in besieging Louvain; the allies then separated and the Dutch recovered another strong fortress, Schenk, on their southern frontier. Rupert's earliest biographer claimed that he 'covered himself with glory' in this campaign and added that 'an active prince as ours was always for charging the enemy; he knew no other cunning or mystery of state than to fight well; believed valour was more the virtue of his age than prudence...'

Rupert's eldest surviving brother, Charles Louis, who was now eighteen, assumed his father's title of Elector Palatine and was invited by his uncle, King Charles I, to pay a visit to England. The invitation was naturally welcomed, for Charles Louis hoped for English assistance in regaining at least the throne at Heidelberg. The young prince, once in England, could perceive that his warmest supporters were to be found among the Puritans who resented the overthrow of a Calvinist ruler by a popish emperor.

Three months later Rupert joined his elder brother at the court of Whitehall. Neither of the brothers took easily to society, for they were shy and inexperienced. Rupert's mother thought that he was still 'a little giddy'. She asked one of the King's officials, Sir Henry Vane the Elder, to give Rupert the benefit of his advice, observing that 'he is good-natured enough, but does not always think of what he should do'. But she was confident that 'he will not trouble your ladies with courting them'. In time he proved himself energetic and vivacious. Another courtier friend of his mother reported that Charles I 'takes great pleasure in his [Rupert's] unrestfulness, for he is never idle; in his sport serious, in his conversation retired, but sharp and witty when occasion provokes him.' He had studied painting and drawing when he was at Leyden so that he was attracted by the King's love of the arts and his splendid collection of Italian and Flemish masters. Queen Henrietta Maria, an enthusiastic Roman Catholic, marked out this nephew of hers as a possible convert, though in that she proved eventually to be dis-appointed.

While Rupert was in England he visited Oxford for the first time, where the honorary degree of Master of Arts was con-ferred upon him. William Laud, the Archbishop of Canterbury, who was also chancellor of the university and a fellow of St John's College, entertained him there; he thought Rupert should enter the Church and might make a good bishop. Another scheme for his future was that he should lead an expedition to occupy and colonize the island of Madagascar off south-east Africa. It was hazarded that 'he that is Lord of Madagascar may in good time be the emperor of India'. How serious the project was is not entirely clear. At any rate towards the end of his stay his mother was informed that 'the dream of Madagascar has vanished'. She must have been relieved to hear this, for she had earlier written to one of her friends in England, 'As for Rupert's romance about Madagascar, it sounds more like one of Don Quixote's conquests when he promised his trusty squire to make him king of an island.' A scheme was also mooted to marry him to a wealthy French heiress, who was said 'to be handsomer than was necessary', but it came to nothing. In the end his mother, his uncle and Archbishop Laud all agreed that he had best become a pro-fessional soldier, which was evidently what Rupert himself wanted. However, Queen Elizabeth was concerned over the reports she received of his life of pleasure. In May 1637 she in-sisted that he should spend the summer with the Dutch army rather than idly in England. Charles and Henrietta Maria were reluctant to let him go, Charles because he enjoyed Rupert's company, Henrietta Maria because she believed she was on the point of gathering in a convert. Rupert himself was reported to have said after going out hunting with his uncle for the last time that 'he wished he might break his neck, and so leave his bones in England'. On his departure Charles gave him a pen-sion of 800 crowns.

After the two brothers returned to Holland, they threw them-selves into a scheme for raising an army of their own to march south and reconquer the Palatinate from the Emperor. But while Charles Louis was negotiating and recruiting in Germany Rupert and his younger brother Maurice went to join Prince

Frederick Henry, who was engaged in besieging the fortified town of Breda on the Dutch frontier, which had been lost to the Spaniards by Maurice of Nassau in 1625. Among the besieging force were to be found several English Protestant officers including Colonel George Goring, son of the future Earl of Norwich, Captain George Monck, a Devonian who was in command of the Colonel's company in the regiment, Henry Hexham, the quartermaster of the regiment, who was to write an invaluable military textbook, and Sir Jacob Astley and Lord Wilmot, who were gentlemen volunteers. Rupert was to be the colleague of Goring, Astley and Monck in the years to come.

The two brothers proved themselves useful. One night, after they had crept up the glacis (a bank sloping down from the fort), they were able to report that the enemy were preparing for a sortie. This intelligence enabled the Dutch forces to be ready before the beleaguered troops could advance across the drawbridge. Soon afterwards Prince Frederick Henry decided to attack a hornwork (an outwork of the fortress, which consisted of two projecting bastions joined by a curtain wall). Mines were driven into the hornwork and Captain Monck was ordered to lead an attack to be delivered through the breach once the mines had exploded. Rupert joined the assaulting party, which took the hornwork after desperate fighting. When Breda fell a month later, Rupert returned to The Hague.

During 1637 and much of 1638 Rupert's elder brother had been collecting soldiers in northern Germany, largely paid for with English money, of which much had been contributed by William Lord Craven, a rich and devoted admirer of Elizabeth of Bohemia. Some reason for optimism existed: although after the death of Gustavus Adolphus in 1632 the imperial armies had recovered the initiative, and the Protestant forces had suffered defeat at the battle of Nordlingen, losing thousands of men, by March 1638 the French and Swedes had concluded a fresh offensive and defensive alliance permitting a series of attacks to be launched on the imperial armies. The Swedish armies, subsidized by the French, had two very able commanders, the young and single-minded Duke Bernard of Saxe Weimar and Marshal Johan Baner, both of whom had learned their trade under Gustavus Adolphus, while the imperial armies lacked good generals. Early in 1638 Bernard had defeated an

13

imperial army near Basel and had then threatened the strategic town of Breisach, while 300 miles to the north-east Marshal Baner won a battle near Chemnitz in Saxony and marched eastwards towards the Elbe to invade Bohemia. The little Palatine army under two youthful princes aimed to advance between these two larger forces through Westphalia and Hesse Cassel, with Heidelberg as their ultimate objective.

Their army consisted of three cavalry regiments, one of which was commanded by Rupert, a regiment of lifeguards, led by the faithful Lord Craven, and a few dragoons and artillerymen. It formed up at Meppen on the river Ems, then marched during the autumn to the valley of the river Weser, where it was joined by a detachment of Swedes sent by Marshal Baner under the command of a Scottish professional officer, James King. Their immediate purpose was to take the wealthy town of Lemgo, reputedly ill defended, which lay south of the Minden gap, Rupert heading the vanguard. As he approached Lemgo, he turned aside to attack an imperial garrison and succeeded in surprising three troops of horse stationed in front of the town. In that rather unnecessary skirmish Rupert was nearly killed by a shot from a 'screwed gun', a kind of rifle. On approaching Lemgo the Palatine army, estimated to number, together with the Swedish contingent, about 4,000 men, was abashed to discover that a much larger army under Count Hatzfeld had been deployed to dispute their passage over the Weser. They decided to retreat back to the safety of the Minden gap. But the route was ill chosen; Hatzfeld caught up with his opponents at Vlotho on the Weser and before their infantry and artillery arrived in support the Palatine cavalry was surrounded. Rupert and his fellow colonels were taken prisoners. After Rupert surrendered and removed his helmet his Austrian captor was surprised to see how youthful the Palatine colonel was.

Opposite A portrait by Van Dyck of the French princess Henrietta Maria, Charles I's queen whose supposed political influence and Roman Catholic zeal were resented by English Protestants.

Rupert was taken through Bavaria and thence to imprisonment in the castle of Linz, a fine building on the river Danube. On his way there he tried in vain to escape, but he did manage to send a message to his uncle in England asking him to obtain his release. However, the Emperor Ferdinand III (who had succeeded his father in February 1637) naturally regarded Rupert as a valuable hostage. To begin with he was closely confined, but he was able to amuse himself with sketching

15

and painting and perfected, we are told, 'an instrument for the drawing of anything into perspective', adapting an invention of Albrecht Dürer. Rupert got along well enough with the governor of the castle, Count Kuffstein, and even better with his daughter, who was reputedly 'one of the brightest beauties of her age'. Her father, who had himself been converted from Lutheranism to Roman Catholicism, attempted, with the aid of a couple of Jesuits, to put his prisoner on the true path. Gradually the severity of Rupert's confinement was relaxed; he was permitted to shoot and play tennis; the English ambassador at Vienna sent him a white poodle which he named Boye and he made a pet of a young hare which followed him everywhere. Later he was even allowed to go hunting outside the castle and received a visit of courtesy from the Archduke Leopold (the Emperor's brother), with whom he was to become close friends.

Eventually King Charles I procured his nephew's release, but Rupert had reluctantly to promise never to fight against the Emperor again. After staying for a time in Vienna, where he was offered a command in the imperial army, he visited his birthplace of Prague and then returned via Saxony to his mother at The Hague. This was at the end of December 1641, a week before Charles I, at loggerheads with his House of Commons, vainly tried to arrest five of its members, including two of his most prominent critics, John Pym and John Hampden, being accompanied on this adventure by Rupert's brother, Charles Louis. Whatever Charles Louis's feelings may have been – and they were mixed – Rupert owed his uncle a debt of gratitude for his release. Even before the Civil War broke out, he came to England.

Rupert crossed the Channel in February 1642, becoming rather sick on the way. At Dover he met his uncle: Charles was there to see off his wife who was going to Holland as a chaperone to their daughter Mary, recently married to William Prince of Orange, the second son of the Dutch captain-general, Frederick Henry. Though the ostensible purpose of Queen Henrietta Maria's journey was to ensure that her daughter was comfortably installed in her new home, she intended in fact to raise money on the crown jewels to buy arms for her husband to use in the civil war which was now felt to be almost unavoidable.

King Charles did not at this stage want to provoke Parliament by welcoming to his court his soldier nephew, who had already earned something of a reputation as a dashing cavalry officer. So he persuaded Rupert to accompany his aunt back to Holland and help her with her shopping. By the early summer the final breach between King Charles I and the parliamentary leaders was brought to a head when Charles firmly refused to relinquish control of the militia, the only armed force in the kingdom, or to allow his ministers and officers to be nominated for him.

After the Queen's departure Charles left London for York, where he was joined by some of the nobility and members of Parliament. Starting to recruit an army, he went to Nottingham in the midlands in pursuit of this aim. In July, Henrietta Maria summoned Rupert from The Hague to meet her and told him that the English king wanted to appoint him his general of horse. Rupert accepted the offer with alacrity, persuaded his Dutch great-uncle to lend him a warship, and after an adventurous trip across the North Sea disembarked with his brother Maurice at Tynemouth whence he at once left for Nottingham. Although the King was not there when Rupert, who had ricked his shoulder in his haste, arrived, Charles returned to perform the ceremony of raising his standard, which signified his declaration of war on Parliament. Rupert was present on this momentous occasion (22 August 1642), and was to serve and fight for his uncle throughout the First Civil War.

Chapter Two

✤

CHARACTER
OF THE
WARFARE

Before examining Rupert's achievements as a commander in the First English Civil War, we must consider the character of the military situation into which he was born and in which he was brought up.

Until modern times the history of warfare consists largely in the changing relationship between attack and defence. As each new weapon has slowly been evolved, the means to withstand it has equally gradually been discovered. In the thirteenth century the earlier invention of the stirrup enabled the Mongolian horsemen to overrun most of the civilized world. In the fourteenth century the longbow, which could fire ten to twelve arrows a minute, neutralized the heavily mailed feudal knight. At the beginning of the sixteenth century the use of gunpowder, first employed by the Chinese in fireworks, permitted fighting with cannon, in siege warfare, giving an advantage to the offence, and the arquebus. But the range and accuracy of missile weapons left much to be desired: in the later half of the century the Spaniards, who were reckoned to be the finest soldiers in Europe, still relied on the pike in conjunction with the musket to win wars. The Spanish tercios originally consisted of huge, closely packed and lengthy rectangles of up to 3,000 pikemen, protected by shot. This was essentially a defensive combination, so heavily armoured that it could hardly be shifted, though in an offensive it could sometimes steamroller its enemy by sheer weight. Pikemen were then able to withstand a cavalry attack – for the cavalry pistols were accurate for only ten yards while the pike outranged the lance and the sword and were ready to move into action as soon as the musketeers had shattered the enemy ranks with their fire.

Maurice Count of
Nassau and Prince of
Orange (1567–1625),
who with Gustavus
Adolphus, King of
Sweden, was one of the
two chief influences
upon Rupert in the
art of war.

The first half of the seventeenth century produced two great
innovators in the art of war: Prince Maurice of Orange and
King Gustavus Adolphus of Sweden. Rupert fought under
neither of them, but he served as an officer with Maurice's
brother, Frederick Henry, in the Dutch war, while his father
had been a volunteer with the army of Gustavus Adolphus in
Germany.

Prince Maurice's contribution to change in warfare was to

19

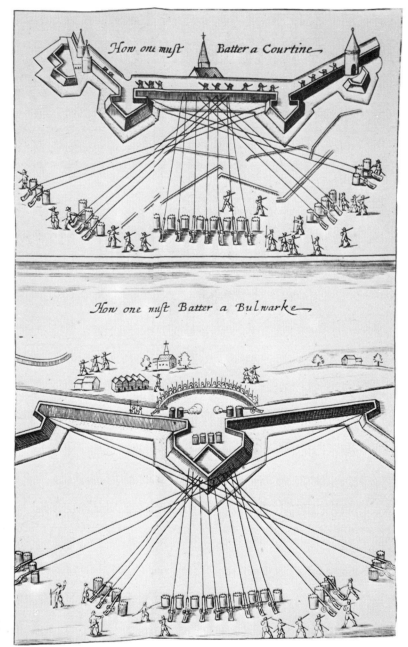

Siege warfare, from
Thomas Venn's
*Military and Maritime
Discipline* (1672).

20

give his troops more flexibility and mobility. He drew up his infantry ten lines deep instead of in the unwieldy Spanish tercios. 'His Highness expressly commandeth', wrote Henry Hexham, 'that no files should be made more than ten deep' – and that applied both when they were on the move and when they were in battle order. Maurice also reduced the proportion of pikemen in the infantry: whereas the Spaniards used twice as many pikemen as musketeers, Maurice equalized them; they fought in divisions or battalions (half a regiment) composed of 250 pikemen and 250 musketeers. Thus he was able to deploy an increased firepower with cavalry support. The cavalry was placed on either side of the infantry to prevent it from being outflanked. Maurice withdrew the lance from the cavalry in 1597 and armed it instead with arquebus, carbine or pistol. His cavalry was arranged in columns with a front of fifteen horsemen who fired their pistols and then wheeled aside to let the next rank take their places, a manoeuvre that was called the 'caracole'. But this kind of missile warfare was not conducive to successful shock tactics if the first salvo was withstood. The defence thus regained the lead that it had lost to cannon in the fifteenth century.

So set battles became scarce and indeed were deliberately avoided by Maurice on the ground that they were likely to be risky and indecisive. Emphasis was laid instead on siege warfare. Maurice persuaded the University of Leyden to add fortification to its studies, which proved of benefit to Rupert when he was there. The fortification of towns was raised to a fine art. The ideal fortified city was shaped as a polygon with walls linking the bastions or demi-bastions and protected by detached or semi-detached outworks. The whole was masked by a glacis so as to prevent the attackers from obtaining a view of the base of the defences; the glacis was a long slope which extended from the parapet of the covered way to meet the natural surface of the ground. Besiegers built encircling lines of trenches starting a mile away from their objective in order to stop the garrison receiving supplies or breaking out. When a breach in the walls had been effected and no relief could be expected the garrison would normally surrender on a summons without facing an assault.

Gustavus Adolphus went much further than Maurice in

Gustavus Adolphus of Sweden emphasized the
importance of mobility and flexibility in warfare as
means to offensive strategy, as distinct from the less
mobile and more defensive methods of the Spanish.

making his army mobile. He reduced the ranks of his infantry from ten to six and sometimes even to three. One reason for this was that if there were too many ranks the rear ranks could not hear a word of command. His men were armed with lighter muskets – the firelock (in which the firing was ignited by sparks) giving way to the matchlock, the musketeers either marched back through their ranks to the rear after they had fired or fired simultaneously in three ranks, one man kneeling, one stooping and the third standing upright. Gustavus Adolphus also increased the proportion of pikemen to musketeers and employed them to charge the enemy after the musketeers had let off a salvo. The length of the pike was shortened: previously it was eighteen feet, now it was about eleven. His cavalrymen were given swords as well as pistols as weapons; only the front rank was allowed to fire before moving into the attack with its swords. Finally the Swedish king used more artillery, introducing 2-pounders and 3-pounders, which could be manhandled or drawn by a single horse so as to keep up with the infantry on the march. It was his combination of all arms in the offensive that gave him his victories at Breitenfeld and Lützen in the Thirty Years' War. There are, however, two legends about Gustavus Adolphus's innovations which have no basis: one is that he abolished the rests which the musketeers had to carry and employ to ensure that their aim was steady; the second concerns his introduction of the so-called 'leather guns' which could be carried on a horse's back. In fact these guns, which were merely covered with leather, were little used and had small significance.

Thus Gustavus Adolphus, by lightening his military equipment and making his formations less cumbersome and more mobile, restored the shock power to the offensive. He himself was a battle-minded warrior, while in sieges he preferred an assault to a long-drawn-out investment. He devoted especial attention to building up his lines of communication with well-defended base areas and carefully distributed supply dumps, and he concerned himself personally with the commissariat. This meant that his armies were manoeuvrable even when far from their homeland. After his victories over the Poles and the Germans seventeenth-century warfare could never be the same again. And although Rupert fought on the side of the

THE PRINCIPLES
OF THE
ART MILITARIE,
Practiſed in the Warres of the United Netherlands:

REPRESENTED BY FIGURE,
THE VVORD OF COMMAND,
AND DEMONSTRATION.

Compoſed by HENRY HEXHAM, Quarter-Maſter to
the Regiment of the Honourable Colonell GORING,
Governour of Portsmouth.

LONDON,
Printed by *Robert Young*, at the ſigne of the Starre
upon Bread-ſtreet-hill,
1639.

Henry Hexham's *Principles of the Art Militarie practised in the warres of the United Netherlands* (1642–3) reflected the increased importance of musketry. Here, two pages showing instructions for musketeers and pikemen. Hexham fought with Rupert at the siege of Breda.

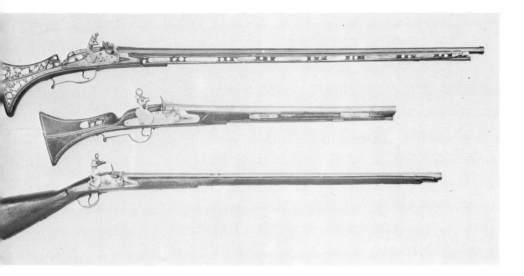

Dutch and not the Swedes, it was essentially Swedish methods that he was to adopt.

The principal officers of the army were the general, the marshal of the field, the general and lieutenant-general of the horse, a general of ordnance, a sergeant-major-general of the foot and a quartermaster-general. Ideally all orders were given in writing, but this was not always feasible. Before taking important tactical decisions these officers would meet in a council of war, and usually the general accepted the advice given to him. The duties of the marshal of the field made him what in later times would be called chief of staff. According to Hexham, he 'is in command and authority next unto the General and is (as it were) his Lieutenant and Mouth'. It was his duty to see that justice was properly administered and he marched at the head of the army along with the sergeant-major-general of the foot, the quartermaster-general and the quartermasters of every regiment. Each company of foot had a captain and a lieutenant; the colonel and major of a regiment had companies larger than the rest which were commanded by deputies. Maurice in fact used the company as his tactical unit. The companies could either operate on their own or be concentrated into battalions, while regiments could be joined together into brigades. In theory an infantry regiment contained about 1,200 men (ten

Three flintlock muskets. The top two date from 1610–20; the one in the centre, perhaps originally a matchlock or fowling gun, had its lock replaced ca. 1650. The third musket is from about 1640–50.

25

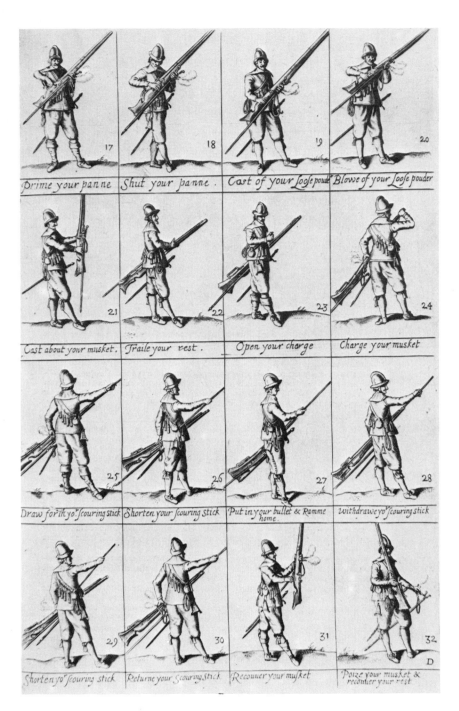

companies). Cavalry regiments, which normally consisted of six troops, were much smaller: though nominally they might contain over 420 men (six troops of seventy each) in fact they were rarely as large as that.

The infantry consisted of a mixture of musketeers and pikemen right down to the company level. Although it was much easier to learn to be a pikeman than to be a musketeer, during the Civil War the number of musketeers was increased at the expense of the pikemen. Undoubtedly that was because pikemen showed themselves to be more vulnerable to cavalry attack, once the caracole had been abolished. But the musket was a clumsy weapon: a long series of commands had to be given both for its loading and unloading. In Henry Hexham's textbook *The Principles of the Art Militarie* (1642–3) are to be found no fewer than forty-eight drawings of different positions, while the pikemen only merit half the number. Because of what proved to be the vulnerability of the pikemen, the usual layout was to station them in the middle with musketeers on each side. The pikemen tended to cut down the length of their weapons because they were so unwieldy, but this made them even more likely to be disrupted by a cavalry charge. The musketeers wore two bandoliers containing their bullets, and carried cord soaked in vinegar as match for the muskets as well as the rests from which they fired. Their rate of fire was one round every three minutes and their estimated range was up to 400 yards. Owing to the time it took to load and unload, when the musketeers came near to their enemy they usually preferred to use their weapons as clubs.

The cavalry was undoubtedly the decisive arm in the Civil War (except in country enclosed by hedges), and came to replace the infantry as 'the queen of the battle'. On both sides cavalrymen were instruments of the offensive; even Gustavus Adolphus's plan of allowing the front rank to fire its pistols, as at Lützen, before it charged, was abandoned. In fact the advance took place with horsemen brandishing their swords; the pistols or carbines were reserved for close fighting after and not before the charge was delivered. The cavalryman normally wore a pot or helmet with a face aperture, and armour on his back and breast over his buff coat. George Monck, who wrote a military textbook in the 1640s, observed that defensive armour and arms were 'much slighted [underestimated] by some in these times', but noted that 'soldiers go into the field to conquer and not be killed'. Incidentally, Monck was against arming horsemen with muskets; he thought that both cavalry and dragoons (mounted infantry) did better to have 'a good Snapance to a Musket Barrel' than a musket. During the Civil War cavalry usually fought in three lines and trotted into battle. That would not have been possible if they had been allowed to halt and fire when they saw the whites of their enemy's eyes, as had previously been customary.

The musketeers had a triple role. First they took their part in the ordinary infantry struggle. Secondly they protected the pikemen against the enemy cavalry; and if their salvo failed to check an enemy advance, they would move into the shelter of the pikemen. Thirdly, following the practice of Gustavus Adolphus, small groups of musketeers actually interspersed with the cavalry, so that they could loose off one salvo while the cavalrymen were getting ready to charge with their swords, and a second one when the cavalry returned from their charge. Monck thought that each division of horse should consist of 120 men ranged three deep and that with each division there should be twelve files of musketeers and twelve files of pikemen at their sides; but, he added, if in battle the horse are without infantry to fight amongst them, then a division of horse should be only ninety men ranged three deep. One objection to interspersing infantry with the cavalry was that it slowed down the rate at which the horse could advance, thus forfeiting one of the principal advantages of cavalry. Nevertheless Monck insisted that 'if you fight Foot among your Horse, your Foot must advance with your Horse and not behind it'.

Another point which Monck stressed was that a good intelligence service was essential. 'A provident commander,' he remarked, 'should try to discover his enemy's designs and to conceal his own.' Good guides and maps were needed not merely on the march but when reconnoitring the enemy's positions. Henry Hexham regarded the marshal of the field as the head of army intelligence: 'he should', he wrote, 'understand of what strength in horse and foot the enemy is and have an exact map of the country.' Unfortunately exact maps were hard to come by and guides could prove unreliable. Junior officers were evidently not trained in intelligence work. Prince Rupert found by experience that it was best for him to undertake his own reconnaissance.

Military historians are by no means in agreement about how valuable artillery was in the seventeenth century. Heavy field guns were estimated to have an effective range of 2,000 yards, but their rate of fire was only ten cannon balls to the hour; the lighter guns had a range of 600 yards, but even 3-pounders could only be fired some fifteen times an hour. The guns had to be hauled over poor roads by oxen or horses; eight horses were required for heavy artillery, three or four for the lighter pieces which were sometimes carried in infantry regiments. Thus the possession of guns reduced the speed at which an army could advance; sometimes, as at the Battles of Edgehill and Preston, they got left behind, and occasionally they were lost. Undoubtedly they were needed for siege-work, but in battle they were most useful for softening up the enemy before an attack. Afterwards they might help to cover a retreat. The heavy artillery made a lot of noise but did little harm. For a salvo a well-deployed company of musketeers was more effective.

It has sometimes been stated that at the outset of the Civil War soldiers did not wear uniforms. But the truth appears to be that each regimental colonel prescribed and supplied his own uniforms, which might have been red, blue or white. However, the cavalry on both sides wore buff, and so were not easily distinguishable. Moreover the infantry on both sides might have happened to be dressed in the same colour uniforms. That was why they wore scarves and handkerchiefs or put green branches or pieces of paper in their hats so that in battle they would not be mistaken by their own comrades for the enemy. At the siege of Breda the Dutch wore scarves of orange and blue, which was distinctive enough; at the Battle of Marston Moor the parliamentarians wore white paper in their hats.

Uniforms, like drill, were an aid to training and discipline. Prince Maurice thought drill and weapon training were the secrets of victory. Gustavus Adolphus's army was originally a national one raised by conscription, but by the time he was killed it was weighted down with mercenaries. A high standard of discipline was needed to blend these various elements, more

The figures of foure seuerall peeces of Ordnance, renforced, cast for the States of the vnited Provinces.
A Falconet of 2100 pound weight, the length 10¼ of a foote.

The Dyamiter of the boore is 2¾ ynches

The Rammer   The Ladle

2 A Feild peece weighing 3200 ℔ weight the length 9 foote and ¾

The Dyamiter of the boore is 4½ of an ynch

(12) ℔ bullet

The Rammer   The scourer or Spunge.

3 A Demy Canon weighing about 4500 ℔ the length 11 foote and ¼.

The Dyamiter of the Boore is 6 ynches

(24) ℔

A Whole Canon weighing about 7000 ℔ weight the length 12½ foote

The Dyamiter of the boore is 7½ ynches (48) ℔

The Scale of an English foote at 12 ynches to the foote

Seventeenth-century
field artillery pieces.

especially as the mercenaries might speak different languages.
But in the Civil War, to begin with at any rate, the rival armies
consisted mainly of militiamen, who had only rudimentary
training, except in London, and of volunteers. Furthermore,
little time was available for training before the first battles were
fought. The royalists had the advantage that most of their

cavalrymen brought their own horses with them and could adapt themselves to military action fairly quickly, although, as Rupert found to his cost, they could not easily be halted and rallied once they had engaged. All the military writers paid lip-service to the importance of training and discipline. But in the Civil War there was not much time to reach a high standard. Such time as there was had to be devoted to weapon training, especially in view of the complexity of the matchlock musket. In the heat of an assault discipline was liable to fall to pieces, as was the case in the royalist attack on Leicester and the parliamentarian assault on Wexford.

All the writers on war stressed the value of morale. George Monck, not a particularly religious man, wrote that 'the first thing that a General should do is to desire God to assist him in all his Counsels and Actions'. Unquestionably most commanders (Wallenstein, the Bohemian tycoon, excepted) went to war in the conviction that their God (whether Protestant or Catholic) was fighting on their side. But to inspire the rank and file, who were usually mercenaries, pressed men or conscripts, with a high sense of duty was not so simple. Indeed, when mercenaries were beaten they often went over to the victorious side. Desertions were frequent.

One reason for this was that the profession of soldiering was not generously paid. As a rule a private in the infantry received 8d a day (when the price of bread was a penny a pound) while the cavalry trooper was given 2s a day. But out of their pay infantrymen had to meet the cost of food and clothing, while the trooper was expected to bring and feed his own horse. Thus no great temptation was offered to make men enlist, unless they were released criminals or poverty-stricken – though at a time of unemployment men would flock to the colours hopeful of pay and plunder. Oliver Cromwell was to prove the most successful general in instilling into his men a sense of purpose similar to his own. Nevertheless, the failure of Parliament to provide regular pay undermined the morale of the New Model Army and embittered its soldiers against their political leaders. At the time when a breach between Parliament and its army took place the privates were said to be a whole year in arrears with their pay. The officers, however, managed pretty well and were quite adequately rewarded. Often they thought it worth their while to buy up their privates' debentures, that is to say their promises-to-pay, as a form of investment or speculation. The royalist soldiers were even worse off since Charles I's principal source of money was borrowing from a few wealthy men, just as the Palatine princes had done from Lord Craven. There too the question of how to maintain morale was hard to solve. At the decisive battle of the First Civil War, at Naseby in the midlands, the Yorkshire infantry were reluctant to fight because they were so far away from their homes.

Rupert, like Gustavus Adolphus, was extremely battle-minded. This was partly owing to the influence of the Swedish king's methods and partly to the special circumstances of the Civil War. Gustavus Adolphus had experimented to find the best way of combining firepower and shock; hence the intermingling of the musketeers with cavalry and the abolition of the caracole. After Breitenfeld, writes Michael Roberts, Gustavus Adolphus 'does not merely seek battle on every favourable occasion; he sees a decision by battle as the logical and consciously designed end to the strategic perspective, and hence as a prime factor influencing the choice of means.' Broadly speaking, most generals – Frederick the Great and Napoleon, for example, both of whom fought many battles – have been shy of engaging in battle unless they were able to concentrate superior forces at vital points and moments. Battles, wrote Sir James Turner, who took part in the Civil Wars, are a great hazard, and a good general should never allow himself to be forced to fight. A battle won, it is true, might bring an end to a war, but a battle lost could be disastrous. On the other hand, the abandonment of a siege or the loss of a town was rarely crucial. Gustavus Adolphus did not have any such inhibitions towards the end of his life, but at the start of his military career he was extremely cautious. Though Rupert was so battle-minded, he did warn Charles I against fighting at Naseby.

On the whole, the best commanders in the Civil War were not unduly afraid of battles. One reason for this was that siege warfare on the continental model, as waged by the Princes of Orange against the Spaniards, and by Anglo-Dutch armies against the French later in the century, was inapplicable to the spirit of the times or to the situation in England. Few strongly fortified towns existed: Bristol twice surrendered rapidly because its garrison commander recognized that it was indefensible against a superior foe. At the same time not much powerful siege artillery was available. For this reason fortified country houses, like Basing House in Hampshire and Lathom House in Lancashire, were able to hold out for a long time. York, which did have stout walls, resisted no fewer than three armies for a period of months. Thus mining – introduced, it is said, by Rupert – came to be preferred to cannonading as a means of capturing strongholds. But mining, being a novel and highly technical device, was tricky.

Such then was the position when the English Civil War opened. Rupert was quick to imbibe the lessons taught by the Dutch war and the Thirty Years' War as well as to profit from his own limited military experiences. Moreover he was a born leader. As Sir Philip Warwick wrote, 'he put that spirit into the King's army that all men might seem resolved.'

Chapter Three

❧

GENERAL OF HORSE:
VICTORIES

After raising his standard at Nottingham and publishing his proclamation of war in which he described the members of Parliament who remained at Westminster as traitors, King Charles honoured his nephew by making him a Knight of the Garter with all due ceremony. At the same time the Prince exacted from his uncle a promise that he should receive his orders as general of horse from him alone, bypassing both Robert Bertie, Earl of Lindsey, a sexagenarian grandee with rather out-of-date ideas about warfare whom Charles had appointed as his general-in-chief, and Patrick Ruthven, Lord Forth, a professional Scottish officer nearly seventy years old whom the King had chosen as his marshal of the field. What these elderly gentlemen thought of the whipper-snapper of twenty-two who had burst in from Holland bringing his own advisers, including his brother Maurice and the experienced engineer Bernard de Gomme, is not recorded.

Charles had a change of heart immediately after raising his standard, possibly because his troops suffered a setback in a skirmish at Coventry. He sent two representatives to London to suggest to the parliamentarians that they should enter into peace negotiations with him. The Houses of Parliament not unreasonably replied that they would not negotiate until the King had taken down his standard and withdrawn his accusation of treason against their members. Rupert, who at this stage naturally regarded the situation in simple terms as a contest between an anointed monarch and his rebellious subjects, was pleased at this answer: the gage had been picked up.

During the next month of September he showed all the impulsiveness of a young man in a hurry. He took over the

The Earl of Lindsey, Charles I's
first general-in-chief.

command of the cavalry from Lord Wilmot, with whom he
had fought in Holland and who now became his second-in-
command, and he began energetically to equip, recruit and
train his troopers. In pursuit of money he rode from Nottingham
to Leicester, where he addressed the mayor in no uncertain language, demanding the sum of £2,000 for the King's service to
be repaid in convenient time, adding by way of postscript to
his letter: 'If any disaffected persons with you shall refuse themselves or persuade you to neglect the command, I shall tomor-
row appear before your town, in such a posture, with horse,
foot and cannon, as shall make you know it is more safe to obey
than resist His Majesty's command.' Charles nervously repudiated his nephew, but it does not appear that he refused the sum
of £500 sent by the mayor to Rupert by way of *douceur*.

Wheras the houne of one Baskaruuile at Baywoth. is by my warrant appoin̄ted for the Quarter of my owne Sargiant Major, Thes̄ ar̄ to will and require all persons — whatsoeuer belonginge to his Ma[ties] Army̅ not to trouble or molest the sayde Baskaruuile, or to offer for to Lodge or quarter any Such men or others in his house or in the particular quarter of Maior legḡ as they shall answer̄ the Con-trary; Giuin this [16]th June 1643

Rupert

A peremptory tone and aggressive signature
characterize Rupert's correspondence during the
Civil War.

Before he left Nottingham Rupert had begun the first of a series of quarrels with George Viscount Digby, son of the Earl of Bristol, who had raised a cavalry regiment for the King. Digby seems to have uttered caustic remarks about the low-class company kept by Rupert (who was never a complete courtier), for he (Digby) produced a somewhat grovelling apology.

Shortly afterwards Rupert wrote a remarkable letter to the Earl of Essex, whom Parliament had commissioned as captain-general of its army (which had by then reached Northampton), offering either to meet him in a pitched battle or to fight a duel with him. Rupert added: 'I know my cause is so just that I need not fear; for what I do is agreeable both to the laws of God and man, in the defence of true religion, a King's prerogative, an uncle's right, a kingdom's safety.' Next time he communicated with Essex, he concluded, it would be on a larger field, using his sword instead of his pen.

After such displays of braggadocio Rupert rejoined the King at Stafford, where he is said to have demonstrated his skill as a marksman by hitting the weather-cock on a church steeple with a bullet from his pistol. The King was then preparing to set up his headquarters in Shrewsbury, a convenient place to gather recruits out of Wales and concentrate soldiers arriving from Ireland via Chester. He also had hopes of gaining control of Worcester, farther south and nearer London. Sir John Byron had brought away gifts of silver plate from the colleges at Oxford, a town which a fortnight later was to be occupied by parliamentarian forces, and carried them to Worcester, accompanied by as many scholars as could obtain horses and arms. Charles asked Rupert to meet Byron there, secure the city and conduct him back to Shrewsbury.

Rupert reached Worcester on 23 September (Byron had been there a week). After surveying the walls and gates of the town the Prince decided it was indefensible against a superior enemy. He encamped with his men, numbering only some 500 horse and 500 foot, just north of Powick Bridge, which crossed the river Teme, a tributary of the Severn, about a mile south of the town. He was not without hopes that he might encounter the vanguard of the parliamentarian army, since it was reported to be marching towards Worcester from Northampton by way of Pershore. His hopes were realized: that afternoon

The parliamentarian captain-general, the Earl of Essex.

a few parliamentarian soldiers, sent forward from the advance guard, approached Powick Bridge in search of intelligence, and were spotted and fired on by royalist musketeers. Aroused from a nap under a hawthorn tree, Rupert, disdaining to call a council of war, ordered his cavalry to charge the enemy, who had crossed the bridge and drawn up in battle order. The numbers on each side were about equal. The horsemen let off their carbines at one another when they were almost nose to nose and then laid to with their swords. The parliamentarians were caught in a narrow lane by officers of daring and experience, including Rupert's brother Maurice, Wilmot and Byron; even the sycophantic Digby was there and fought bravely enough. Most of them except Rupert himself were wounded in the hand-to-hand fighting, but suddenly the parliamentarians melted away, riding at full speed, hatless and with their

39

swords still drawn, back over the bridge to the safety of Pershore.

The King, who was en route from Shrewsbury to Chester on the day of the fight, thought that Worcester would quickly be occupied effectively by his side and commanded Rupert to withdraw to Bridgenorth (halfway between Worcester and Shrewsbury) once that had been done, so that if the Earl of Essex attempted to cut off the royal return from Chester Rupert would be able to stop him. Three days later (25 September) Charles wrote advising Rupert to ensure that Worcester was secure, but ordering him to preserve his forces ready for a battle. He congratulated his nephew on his victory and promised that he would bring reinforcements from Chester. But all that was over-optimistic, for Rupert did not yet have a sufficient number of men at his disposal to withstand a siege of Worcester and had no wish to run the risk of being trapped there. Before the end of September Essex, with his army of some 15,000 men, had therefore been able to occupy Worcester as a base, while the royalists gathered in strength fifty miles north at Shrewsbury, where they remained for a fortnight consolidating and training their growing army. Morale on both sides was high, the royalist because of Rupert's victory, the parliamentarian because they rightly believed that they greatly outnumbered their enemy. So a trial by battle was imminent. Such a battle, everyone thought, would settle the war.

Rupert, who had won a name for himself at Powick Bridge – though he was soon to suffer a rebuff at Coventry – showed himself to be arrogant, tactless, impatient and touchy at Charles's itinerant court. Though he might have preferred mixing with 'low company', a habit he is said to have picked up at The Hague, he emphasized his leadership and princely authority by going about 'clad in scarlet very richly laid in silver lace and mounted on a gallant Barbary horse'. His reputation with the parliamentarians became fantastic. His poodle, Boye, which he had brought with him to England, was believed to jump in the air at the word 'Charles' and cock his leg when his master said 'Pym'. The dog was also thought capable of making himself invisible so as to be able to pass through the enemy lines and report back the intelligence he had gathered to Rupert. Later the legend took a different turn. For the Prince

Rupert's quarters at Wormleighton, Warwickshire, the night before the battle of Edgehill.

himself, though said to be usually 'sparkish' in dress, earned a reputation as a master of disguises enabling him to mingle with parliamentarian soldiers in village taverns.

Marching at the rate of ten miles a day the King's army, after leaving Shrewsbury and penetrating the Birmingham area, reached southern Warwickshire on 22 October 1642. Rupert spent the night at Wormleighton, about eight miles east of the market town of Kineton. When he and his men rode into Wormleighton, his quartermasters ran into quartermasters from the other side, which showed them how near the enemy were. Rupert promptly sent out a reconnaissance unit and that evening was able to inform the King, who was spending the night at Edgecote, five miles south-east of Wormleighton, that the Roundheads had arrived from Worcester and were stationed in force in and around Kineton. The object of the royalist march from Shrewsbury had been to threaten London, but it was of course realized that the Earl of Essex would try to cut them off, so a battle was to be expected. Earlier on 22 October a resolution had been taken at the royalist council of war to occupy Banbury the next day, and after that to push on south by way of Oxford. But at the same time it was not known how close Essex's army was. Rupert advised the King to deploy his army early next morning on Edgehill, which barred two roads south from Kineton, and challenge his enemy to battle. Charles replied at four o'clock in the morning of Sunday 23 October: 'Nephew, I have given order as you have desired so that I doubt not but all the foot and cannon will be at Edgehill betimes this morning where you will also find your loving uncle and faithful friend.'

Both armies placed the infantry in the centre, the cavalry on the wings and dragoons lining the extreme end of each flank. Before the battle Essex's army had been widely scattered, and because Essex was surprised by the proximity of the royalists not all his cavalry and artillery were available to him. To stiffen his infantry he kept two cavalry regiments, those of Sir William Balfour and Sir Philip Stapleton, as reserves at its rear. Because of that, and since in any case Essex had fewer cavalrymen than the royalists, he was outnumbered on both wings.

It is sometimes said that it was because Rupert, taking advantage of his direct access to the King's ear, had interfered with the drawing up of the army that Lindsey now resigned as general-in-chief and instead insisted on serving as a volunteer at the head of his own infantry regiment. But that was not the case: what had upset Lindsey was that Charles had ordered his marshal of the field, the aged Lord Forth, to devise the plan of battle. Forth followed the Swedish procedure of placing the musketeers in a somewhat complicated formation so as to protect the pikemen on all sides. Rupert took charge of the cavalry on the right wing, Lord Wilmot, his second-in-command, of the left wing, and Lord Forth of the infantry in the centre. It had at first been hoped that Essex would attack uphill; but when, because he wanted to brand the royalists as aggressors, he refused to do so, the King's army moved down off the hill. Trumpets and cannonfire signalled the order for the advance.

Before the battle began, as Sir Richard Bulstrode, who served in one of the infantry regiments, recorded: 'Prince Rupert passed from one wing to the other, giving positive orders to the horse to march as close as was possible, keeping their ranks with sword in hand, to receive the enemy's shot without firing either carbine or pistol till we broke in amongst the enemy, and then make use of our fire-arms as need should require.' As the cavalry were deployed in three lines and the infantry in six, the royalist tactics were closely modelled on the Swedish pattern, except that Rupert did not allow even his front rank to employ its fire-arms before the charge, as Gustavus Adolphus had done, nor did he interlard his cavalry with musketeers.

The parliamentarian cavalry, however, did have musketeers stationed with it and the troopers discharged their carbines as Rupert's men advanced upon them. These did little damage, while under Rupert's leadership the royalist cavalrymen moved from a walk into a trot, forced the parliamentarian troopers to retire, and then cut up the exposed and unprotected muske-teers. The same thing happened on the other wing and all the royalist cavalry swept forward onto the parliamentarian base of Kineton where they seized their enemy's wagons and on the way captured some of their guns. While most of their cavalry were thus thrust back the parliamentarian infantry in the centre stood firm and Essex threw in his two reserve cavalry regiments in its support. As Bulstrode wrote, 'the King's horse being all gone off, his foot is charged in the flank by a part of the enemy's horse which put them in disorder.'

Rupert was roundly criticized both by Bulstrode and by later military historians for allowing the pursuit to continue as far as Kineton, two miles to the rear of the battlefield, thus leaving the foot 'naked'. It is absurd to imagine that men like Rupert and Wilmot were greedy for spoil. What evidently happened was that the success of the cavalry charge on both wings spread the conviction that the whole of the parliamentarian army had panicked and was in retreat. In fact the struggle between the pikemen, the musketeers fighting with their butt-ends, and some infantrymen merely armed with cudgels was extremely fierce. Both the Earl of Lindsey and the King's knight marshal, who carried the royal standard, were killed.

By the time the royalist cavalry had returned to the field evening was coming on, ammunition had been spent, and both sides were exhausted. The parliamentarians passed the night on the stricken field and then withdrew to Warwick, while the royalists returned to their original positions on the hill. On 27 October they occupied Banbury and on the 29th they triumphantly entered Oxford from which the parliamentarian garrison had withdrawn. Edgehill was unquestionably a royalist victory, for Essex had been intercepted and pushed back north so that the road to the capital lay open.

Rupert tried hard to persuade the King and the council of war to allow him to take command of a flying column and advance on Westminster before Essex could possibly get there. Clearly the parliamentarian army was demoralized. At first optimistic reports about the result of the battle circulated in London, but the King's occupation of Reading, only forty miles west of the capital, soon generated the gravest forebodings. The sudden appearance of Rupert outside the House of Commons might conceivably have ended the war. But Rupert was overruled, for Charles feared that his impetuous nephew would upset the political apple-cart.

After the death of the Earl of Lindsey at Edgehill, King Charles appointed Lord Forth as general-in-chief. This aged gentleman was a figure out of the past. Gustavus Adolphus had dubbed him 'field-marshal of the bottles and glasses as he could drink immeasurably and preserve his understanding to the last'. In practice Forth acted as Charles's chief of staff while Rupert was given the task of consolidating the defences around Oxford and Reading preparatory to moving on London.

After Essex's return to the capital, when the truth was known about the battle of Edgehill, some members of Parliament were anxious to re-open negotiations with the King, though at the same time a proposal to invite the Scots into England in support of Parliament's cause was under active consideration. Moreover the terms offered by Parliament to the King were stiff. Some of his advisers were to be punished, his ministers were to be chosen for him, and a reformation of the Church of England was to be left for ultimate decision by Parliament. The Roundheads were driven towards negotiation not only by the consequences of Edgehill but by the victories then being achieved on the King's behalf in the north and the west of England. Charles hesitated, playing for time; he was certainly not prepared to yield on the kind of terms then offered to him.

Prince Rupert was impatient about all this. He wanted to thrust towards London – believing, reasonably enough, that his uncle could then dictate his own terms. He tried to capture both Aylesbury and Windsor Castle, which lay between the royalists' base and the north-west and west of London. Eventually the King himself left Reading for Colnbrook, which lies between Windsor and Brentford, north of the Thames. Charles was evidently irritated that when he had offered to come to Windsor Castle to negotiate he had been refused, and he now ordered his nephew to attack Brentford so as to clear the way to his capital and bring pressure upon Parliament. This Rupert did brilliantly, surprising two infantry regiments on a misty day, 12 November.

Encouraged by the victory Charles was at last ready to push on to London. But at Turnham Green he was confronted by a large if disorganized army including the well-trained London militia regiments, while his right flank was menaced by troopers under General Sir James Ramsey concentrated at Kingston five miles to the south. Charles then bowed to the logic of the situation. Neither side was eager to fight. A few cannon shots were exchanged; the Earl of Essex was allowed to re-occupy Brentford and the King slowly withdrew to Reading. Rupert is described as sitting disconsolately on his horse in the Thames at Brentford as he watched his troopers withdrawing over the bridge 'cheering and encouraging the retiring ranks to keep order and fire steadily on the advancing foe'.

A week later Rupert was at Abingdon, south of Oxford, which he used as the headquarters for the royal cavalry and dragoons. Rupert busied himself in organizing provisions for his soldiers and hay, oats and straw for his horses. The officers had to pay for their food and lodging, while half the troopers' pay was docked to meet the cost of their rations. Rupert, remarked one of his biographers, was 'the most zealous of foragers, although he appropriated the best of his collections to his own cherished troopers'.

As winter approached, Rupert's chief difficulties were with his officers. Lord Wilmot, who had been appointed Rupert's lieutenant-general of horse, protested over his orders, saying that proper arrangements were not being made for the quartering of men and horses and that troops were being sent out without any care or design. This was to be a continuing conflict. Sir John Byron, whose cavalry regiment was stationed at Reading, asked to be relieved, as there was neither accommodation nor subsistence for his men. Another officer, in command of Rupert's own cavalry regiment, reported from Abingdon that in one company both the officers and the men had disobeyed orders to march into Buckinghamshire and observed that he himself would rather be Rupert's groom in Oxford than try to cope with such insubordination. Sir Jacob Astley, who was stationed at Reading, was soon complaining that unless his regiment was given its pay or allowed to live on free quarter it could not subsist. Finally Sir Lewis Dyve, who had been appointed governor of Abingdon, grumbled over the shortage of clothes and boots for the troopers and lack of money to pay for shoeing their horses. Though Rupert himself was billeted in comparative comfort at Christ Church, Oxford, he quickly learned that the life of a general of horse was by no means a happy one.

At the beginning of 1643 peace negotiations were resumed. It was hoped on both sides that it might at least be possible to agree on an armistice during which a conference on wider issues might be held, but though elaborate discussions went on for more than two months no agreement was reached because neither the King nor John Pym, who directed the strategy of Parliament, was ready to forgo military advantages. Broadly, the position was that the parliamentarians controlled the capital and most of south-east England – the richest part of the country – and so long as they did so and remained undefeated in a major battle they were strongly placed. On the other hand, the Cornish royalists in the west, and the Yorkshiremen in the West Riding under Charles's friend, the wealthy Marquis of Newcastle, were both winning victories for the King.

Charles's strategic need was to maintain full contact both with his supporters in the north and with those in the south-west, while the aim of the Earl of Essex and his army was to confine the King and his main body to the Oxford area. Sir William Waller, a Devonshire country gentleman who was a more skilful general than Essex (with whom he did not get along very well), held both Bristol and Gloucester, and so long as he did so royalist communications with Wales, their principal recruiting ground, were in danger. Furthermore the capture of Lichfield by the Roundheads at the beginning of March interrupted communications with Yorkshire. Since the Queen had at this very time returned from Holland with arms and money to succour her husband and had established contact with the Marquis of Newcastle in York, it was vital for this route to be cleared. Thus the King's plan was to strengthen his hold on the west midlands so as to clear the way for his wife's arrival, and also to thrust forward into Gloucestershire so as to safeguard his supplies and his recruiting. Meanwhile Essex aimed to distract the royalists from these objectives by threatening Oxford itself from the west.

Prince Rupert was the King's chief lieutenant in carrying out his strategical intentions. As early as 6 January the King had ordered him to assist the Marquis of Hertford in taking the town of Cirencester in Gloucestershire, by covering the siege with his cavalry while Hertford surrounded the town. But Hertford was a man of books, not a military commander, the Cirencester garrison was defiant, and the time of year was not conducive to an assault. Three weeks later, however, the Prince himself took full charge of the operation. He arranged a well-planned rendezvous with another force from Oxford. After misleading the garrison by feinting at nearby Sudeley Castle he surprised the town at break of day on 2 February. The password for the day was 'Rupert' and the attack was a complete success. Charles was delighted for, as he told Rupert, there was much cloth in Cirencester and in the neighbourhood (it was an important weaving centre), and they badly needed cloth for the royalist soldiers' uniforms. Moreover a large quantity of arms was captured, which the King said must be used to equip his old regiments and not distributed among any new levies that might be raised in Gloucestershire. One of the King's secretaries of state, Sir Edward Nicholas, hastened to inform Rupert that his victory would be helpful during the continuing armistice negotiations.

More significantly, the route through Gloucestershire now lay open. But an attempt by Lord Herbert, who had raised a small Welsh army for the King, to take Gloucester itself was easily frustrated by Waller, and when on 8 March Rupert himself marched towards Bristol, having notified that two merchants in the port were willing to betray it, the plot was discovered and the conspirators were hanged. Thereupon Rupert returned to Oxford, where the King at once entrusted his nephew with the duty of expanding the territory under his control to the north and north-east of Oxford so as to clear the way for the coming of the Queen.

After his success at Cirencester Rupert was in high favour with the King. On 12 March Charles wrote to him: 'I mean not to trust you by halfs.' He therefore gave Rupert leave to appoint a governor of Shrewsbury and to include Cheshire within the scope of his command. As to the importance of Newark, a strategic point lying between East Anglia and the East Riding of Yorkshire, where the Marquis of Newcastle was supreme, Charles said that he was sure that his nephew would understand what he wanted him to do (namely, to seize it for his side), 'for an earnest desire to you is as much as a peremptory command to others'. In effect, Rupert, besides being general of horse, had been given an independent command which comprised all the counties that lay around Oxford stretching as far north-west as Cheshire and as far north-east as Nottinghamshire.

As soon as the campaigning season opened in the spring Rupert marched into Warwickshire and assaulted Birmingham which, though a small place, was already a centre of arms manufacture. It put up little resistance and against Rupert's wishes was set on fire. Five days later he summoned Lichfield to surrender: it had been occupied a month earlier by a parliamentarian force. The cathedral and the close had been fortified. The capture of the town presented difficulties, since most of Rupert's troops consisted of cavalry and he had only light guns unsuited to siege work. However, the Prince persuaded his cavalrymen to dismount and fight with the infantry, while he collected coal miners to assist in demolishing the walls as soon as the moat was breached and dried. A first attempt to scale the walls was beaten off, and even after a mine was exploded on the evening of 18 April – the first, it was said, to have been used for military purposes in England – a storming party was thrust back by musket fire. Eventually Rupert got hold of some heavy artillery, which fired through the breach created by the

Ioyfull Newes

FROM

LICHFIELD,

BEING

The true Copie of a Letter ſent from a
Captain in LICHFIELD to his wife in
London, Dated April 17.

Wherein is contained the proceedings of Prince Rupert
againſt the Parliaments Forces in the ſaid town :

CONTAINING

1 *The manner of Prince Ruperts aſſaulting Lichfield.*
2 *His endeavouring to undermine the wall with pick-axes.*
3 *How he attempted to ſcale the wals of the cloſe, and what men
he loſt in that attempt.*
4 *How he was repulſed by the Parliaments Forces, and how they
rung the bels in defiance of him.*
5 *A Poſtſcript annext to this Letter, declaring Prince Ruperts
death upon great probabilities.*

Publiſhed at the deſire of thoſe that upon occaſion will juſtifie the
truth of what is herein contained.

LONDON,
April 22 Printed for *Thomas Watſon.* 1643.

A mendacious
broadsheet printed
immediately after
Rupert's successful
siege of Lichfield in
April 1643, written by
a parliamentarian
officer.

mine. Three days later the cathedral surrendered. So the Prince
fulfilled the first part of his task and opened the route from York
to Oxford for the Queen.

In Rupert's absence from Oxford the Earl of Essex had laid
siege to Reading. The King, therefore, ordered his nephew to
return to Oxford as soon as the siege of Lichfield was completed

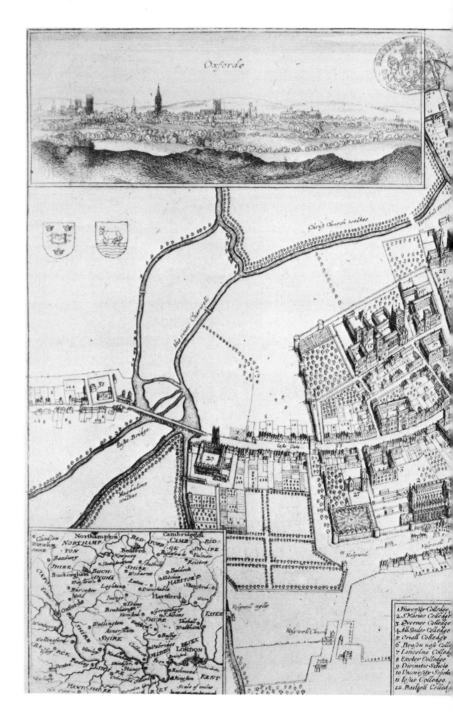

OXFORDE

Blacke Friers

Graye Friers

Litle gate

Paradise

the Castle
Prison

Toward S Northgate

25. S. Ebbes
26. S. Peters in the Baily
27. S. Peters in the Easte
28. S. Michaelis
29. S. Magdalena
30. S. Giles
31. S. Clemens
32. S. Thomas
33. Ladies Chapell
34. Somtime Ofney Abbey
35. White Friers
36. Glocster Hall

37. Highe Bridge
38. Highe Streate
39. South Streate
40. North Streate
41. Corne market
42. Great Baily
43. Quater Voys
44. Castle Streate
45. Castle Streate
46. S. Johns Streate
47. Bridewell
48. Christ Church Knite houses

Oxford in 1643.

51

John Hampden, the puritan statesman and parliamentarian infantry colonel, mortally wounded in a skirmish with Rupert at Chalgrove Field in Oxfordshire on 18 June 1643.

instead of going forward from Newark to join the Queen. But by the time Rupert had got back and met the King at Caversham, north of Reading, the town had surrendered. The governor, Sir Arthur Aston, a veteran of many wars, had been hit on the head by a tile, and the deputy governor, Sir Richard Feilding, who was outnumbered, sued for peace, which he was granted on terms that enabled the garrison to march out with all the honours of war. Feilding was subsequently court-martialled and condemned to death for the surrender, but Rupert interceded on his behalf and he was taken down from the scaffold.

Rupert was irritated by a sense of defeatism and lack of purpose that he detected in Oxford, and was obviously dissatisfied at being recalled from his promising northward advance. Sir Edward Nicholas did his best to soothe him and wrote assuring him that 'the King is much troubled to see your Highness discontented'. In the same letter Nicholas himself added: 'I could wish that some busybodies would not meddle as they do with other men's offices, and that the King would leave every officer respectively to look to his own proper charge, and that his Majesty would content himself to overlook all men to see that each did his duties in their proper places, which would give abundant satisfaction...'

Rupert amused himself by undertaking sorties into the neighbouring countryside to seize food and forage and kept his eyes on his cavalry stationed at Abingdon.

The Earl of Essex, after garrisoning Reading, occupied Thame, thirteen miles west of Oxford, on 10 June and sent an advance guard as far as Wheatley, though it does not appear that his intention was to launch a direct attack on Oxford. Rupert favoured harrying Essex whose forces, though big, were widely scattered. In mid-June the Prince heard a report that a large sum of money was being conveyed from London to Thame and he resolved to intercept it. For this purpose he rode out of Oxford across Magdalen Bridge on 17 June with a force consisting chiefly of cavalry. He missed the convoy but in withdrawing ran into a Roundhead contingent at Chalgrove to the west of the Chiltern hills. As they realized they were outnumbered the parliamentarian dragoons drew up behind a hedge, hoping to hold off their enemy until reinforcements could reach them from Thame. But Rupert himself leapt over the hedge and bore down upon the Roundheads, among whom was the parliamentarian stalwart, John Hampden, an infantry colonel. The parliamentarians broke and fled; prisoners were taken; Hampden was mortally wounded and rode back to Thame to die. His last words were said to have been 'O Lord, save my country!' His loss was a grave blow to Parliament, for he might have been the ideal successor to John Pym, who was to die of cancer before the year was out.

The military situation of the royalists was never again to be so hopeful as it was in the summer of 1643. On 30 June Lord Fairfax and his son were defeated in a battle on Adwalton Moor near Bradford and after that the whole of Yorkshire except Hull fell into royalist hands; Cromwell failed to persuade the local militia to assist him in an attack on Newark in Nottinghamshire; the Earl of Essex withdrew from Thame to Aylesbury, while Rupert, by establishing himself at Buckingham, obliged the parliamentarian commander-in-chief to move away into north Bedfordshire. Because of all this Queen Henrietta Maria was able to leave Yorkshire and reach her husband safely with a small army of her own by way of Lincoln, Newark, Ashby-de-la-Zouch in Leicestershire and King's Norton in Warwickshire. On 7 July Charles appointed Rupert as his commander-in-chief 'to repair with part of his forces for the more secure coming of our dearest consort, the Queen, in her passage to us'. Rupert met Henrietta Maria at Stratford-on-Avon on 11 July and two days later she rejoined her husband at Edgehill. One of the first things the Queen was asked to do was to reconcile Rupert with his second-in-command, Lord Wilmot, since they were still on bad terms.

A week after the Queen's return Prince Rupert set out at the head of a sizeable army, consisting chiefly of infantry, with a view to taking either Bristol or Gloucester or both, thereby clearing the communications between Oxford and South Wales and the west of England. This was the strategic aim of the King – not, as is often said, a converging movement on London. Rupert was able to set about his task with equanimity because the royalist Cornishmen under the guidance of the courageous Ralph Hopton had inflicted three defeats on the parliamentarians at Stratton (16 May), Lansdown (5 July) and Roundway Down (13 July). In the last of these battles, in which Rupert's brother Maurice took a useful part, the army under Waller was virtually annihilated. He retired to Gloucester to lick his wounds. Because of Waller's presence in Gloucester Rupert resolved to attack Bristol, which was under the command of Sir Nathaniel Fiennes, an amateur soldier, whom Rupert had beaten before at Powick Bridge.

Bristol, being 'built in a hole' and surrounded by rocky heights, was not an easy place to defend, but it was a big town, the second largest port in England, and its walls had a circumference of five miles. Thus a substantial army was needed to assault it. Rupert had some 8,000 men, to whom he added Maurice and his Cornishmen who had occupied Bath after their victories over Waller. On Sunday 23 July Rupert and Maurice climbed Clifton church tower, west of the city, to survey the fortifications. A council of war was held and it was agreed to storm the town simultaneously from the south and the west at daybreak on the 25th. The signal was to be the firing of two demi-cannons (which had balls weighing thirty-two pounds).

Whether because they imagined they had heard the signal before in fact it was given or because they wanted the first share in the glory of the action, the Cornishmen anticipated the time of assault and began their attack at three o'clock in the morning. But they were not successful. It was Rupert's infantry which first forced its way into the city. The fight was a hard one, but cavalry as well as infantry were able to enter by the Frome gate on the north-west. Rupert's own horse was killed under him; yet, as an eye-witness reported: 'his Highness having recovered another horse, rode up and down from place to place, where most need was of his presence, here directing and encouraging some, and there leading up others; generally it is confessed by the commanders that had not the Prince been there, the assaults, through mere despair, had been in danger to be given over in many places.'

One is left with the impression from this account that Rupert was in full charge of the operation. Finding that the Cornishmen were held up, he sent for Maurice with a thousand men to reinforce the western attack; but by the time his brother was in position Fiennes had surrendered. Terms of capitulation were soon agreed in writing, including a clause that the inhabitants of the town should be secured from violence. But inevitably plundering took place, though Rupert tried to prevent it. As Fiennes himself wrote, the two princes 'did ride among plunderers with their swords hacking and slashing them', and Rupert apologized for the lawlessness of his men.

While Rupert was at Bristol the Earl of Essex had plucked up courage to move back to Aylesbury, which sufficiently alarmed Charles I to make him tell Rupert to send back some of his cavalry, as they would not be needed at a siege. However, when Charles learned of the swift capture of Bristol he decided to join Rupert in the hope of conquering the whole of the west. He gave orders that everything was to be done to prevent Waller from recruiting more men for his broken army; he recalled the worthy Marquis of Hertford, who had been in command in the west, and ordered Maurice, hitherto in charge only of the horse, to take over from him. He asked Rupert to raise money, to make the best use of the captured ammunition, and to try to add to the royalist forces. The next objective was to be Gloucester.

55

Chapter Four

✤

GENERAL OF HORSE:
DEFEATS

It has often been said that once the First Civil War got under way King Charles's strategic plan for victory was to march on his capital. But when, after an unnecessary delay, Rupert was allowed to do so in November 1642, only to be met by firm resistance from Londoners at Turnham Green, Charles called off the operation and it was never attempted again. If ever there was a time when it might have been successfully carried out it was surely after the fall of Bristol at the end of July 1643. For the royalists had been victorious in Yorkshire, Cornwall, Devonshire, Dorset and Wiltshire; even in East Anglia, a Puritan stronghold, the Roundheads had made little progress. Yet at a council of war summoned after the capture of Bristol, in spite of pressure from some of his advisers to advance on London, the King decided to devote himself to the siege of Gloucester in order to clear his communications with Wales and the west.

Where did Rupert stand on this question? We do not know, but Queen Henrietta Maria believed that at this stage he opposed an immediate move on the capital (which she herself thought desirable). It may well be that Rupert felt that the threat to Gloucester would compel the Earl of Essex to risk a battle – as indeed he was to do – and that the defeat of the main parliamentarian army in the field was a necessary prelude to an assault upon London. That is no doubt what Gustavus Adolphus would have thought.

Gloucester's defence was in the hands of Edward Massey, an officer of enterprise and some experience, and exactly the same age as Rupert. At first Massey was pessimistic and conveyed the impression to the royalists that he would surrender as

quickly as the commander at Bristol had done. After all, he had served the King earlier in his career and might change sides. In fact he was a rigid Presbyterian and anti-Catholic so it is unlikely that he had any such intention. King Charles, who himself took charge of the siege, refused to order a direct assault on the city, partly because he hoped Massey might betray it and partly because he was shocked by the loss of lives among officers and men during the storming of Bristol. Still, war cannot be waged in kid gloves. Rupert had favoured an immediate assault, but was overruled by the numerous other generals on the spot. Major-General Sir Arthur Aston had explained the military difficulties to Rupert three days before the King summoned the town to surrender. He said that the governor of Gloucester would not yield until he had been 'put to some distress'; that the King had not enough infantry at his disposal; therefore the cavalrymen were being kept on perpetual duty, for which they were unsuited as the country round Gloucester was full of hedges and enclosures; finally he added that the country was ill affected to the King and the local clothiers were supplying the garrison with money.

Gloucester was summoned on 10 August, but it was not until 22 August that the Earl of Essex led out of Hounslow an army

A contemporary cartoon. The 'pudel' is probably a reference to Rupert's dog Boye.

57

of 15,000 men (including six regiments of the London trained bands, who had volunteered for the service) to relieve Colonel Massey. Essex took an extremely circuitous route via Uxbridge, Beaconsfield, Aylesbury, Brackley, Bicester, Chipping Norton and Stow-on-the-Wold. Thus he marched twenty miles north of Oxford, whence Wilmot and the royalist cavalry vainly tried to impede his progress. On 4 September, when Essex reached Stow-on-the-Wold, Rupert launched a cavalry attack, but he was outnumbered and repulsed. During the four-week siege the King and Rupert actually left the camp near Gloucester to return to Oxford for a couple of days. It was the first of only two brief occasions when the King's two finest generals met one another, for the heroic Earl of Montrose had come to Gloucester to warn the King of the dangers from the Scottish covenanters with whom John Pym was negotiating a military alliance. Montrose rode with Rupert and Charles as far as Oxford, but did not succeed in impressing the threat of the situation in Scotland on the King, who was content to await the immediate outcome in England. The main reason for his return to Oxford was to soothe his queen who, as has been noted, wanted him to leave Gloucester for London and blamed Rupert because her husband refused to do so.

Before Essex arrived at Gloucester and let Massey know that he had come to his relief, Charles told Rupert that Lord Forth was 'of the opinion that we shall do little good on this town [Gloucester] for they begin to contain us, which will make it a work of time; wherefore he [Forth] was of the opinion, in which I fully concur, that we shall endeavour to fight with Essex as soon as may be . . . the greatest care will be to meet him before he reaches the hedges' – where of course the royalist superiority in cavalry would not count.

Essex entered Gloucester in triumph on 8 September, but after relieving it he had to return immediately to London. The aim of the royalists was to fight Essex somewhere in the Cotswolds where their cavalry would prove invaluable and where they would be in touch with their base at Oxford.

The King assumed that Essex would return by the same route as that by which he had come, and Essex sustained this belief by feinting at Worcester from Tewkesbury, to the north of Gloucester. Charles moved north-east to Pershore, Evesham and Broadway with a view to cutting Essex off from Worcestershire. Thereupon Essex smartly struck south and entered Cirencester, which Rupert had captured with such difficulty at the beginning of the year; then, having found a supply of provisions there, the parliamentarians raced on towards Cricklade and Swindon in Berkshire, intending to reach London by way of Hungerford and Newbury. Rupert with his cavalry searched everywhere for the enemy; as soon as he learned where Essex was, he returned to inform the King and Lord Forth. Eventually he found them installed in a house near Broadway absorbed in a leisurely game of piquet.

Rupert told the King that he proposed to try to cut off Essex's cavalry from his infantry. To this end, on 18 September he delivered an attack at Aldbourn Chase south-east of Swindon, but was beaten off. Nevertheless this attack had its value: it slowed down the march of Essex's army, which was already in difficulties because the roads were muddy through recent rain, while he was running out of the food supplies that had been impounded at Cirencester. The result was that Rupert, riding north through Wantage, reached Newbury first. When the Earl arrived he discovered that Rupert had got there two hours ahead of him and had already occupied the town. Thus the road to London was blocked; Essex would have to try to break through.

Having brought up the infantry and artillery to join Rupert, King Charles, who always vacillated between optimism and pessimism, resolved to fight a battle on the following day. When he left Gloucester he had felt extremely pessimistic; now, with fresh troops (which had been sent from Oxford) at his disposal, he believed that a decisive victory was within his grasp. Rupert has often been accused of foolhardiness; on this occasion, having compensated for the slow and ill-judged march of the King by interposing his cavalry between Essex and London, he was against an immediate battle. He knew that the royalist army was short of powder and ammunition (which could be brought over from Oxford) and that the cavalry would be handicapped by the hillocks and hedges around Newbury in which the parliamentarian commander could deploy most of his infantry. Delaying tactics, he thought, might cause the Roundhead army to break up. His advice was ignored. According to one of his biographers, 'Ever since the arrival of the Queen and her servants, Rupert's influence seems to have been declining, and he was now overruled.'

In retrospect the First Battle of Newbury can be seen as a turning point in the Civil War, for never again was the main army of Charles I to be offered such an excellent opportunity to defeat the parliamentarians in the field and then push on to London. Newbury was essentially a soldiers' battle and much about it is obscure. Its course was dictated by the nature of the terrain. The parliamentarian army was deployed roughly on a three-mile front facing east and running between the river Kennet and the En brook. Two thirds of its line was situated on a flat meadow, but the lower third was positioned on a plateau rising to 400 feet. Both the meadow and the plateau contained many enclosures; it was therefore better suited to infantry than to cavalry action. Essex's army was stronger in infantry, for the London trained bands proved doughty fighters; the royalists were better furnished with cavalry, which Rupert commanded.

By the time the battle began, early in the morning of 20 September, the parliamentarians had succeeded in occupying the crest of the plateau and placing two light guns upon it. The royalist line stretched from Newbury itself south to Wash Common (near where the Falkland memorial now stands) facing the parliamentarians at a distance of about 1,000 yards. In the south both sides tried to outflank the other, while the battle began with an advance by the royalist infantry in the centre.

The fighting was fierce, both musketeers and artillerymen expending a great deal of ammunition. The royalist footsoldiers were soon in trouble and appealed for help from the cavalry. But it was not cavalry country. As deadlock was developing on the meadow Rupert and Sir John Byron, who commanded an infantry brigade, vainly tried to capture the enemy's guns and push them off the plateau. In an attempt to thrust through a narrow gap in a high quick hedge Lord Falkland, one of the King's two secretaries of state, who was serving as a volunteer in Byron's brigade, was killed; Byron's horse was killed under him, while Rupert, who also led a brigade, was eventually compelled to retire before the steady fire of the enemy musketeers. By the time darkness fell the royalists had almost run out of

Lord Falkland, one of
Charles's secretaries of
state, who was killed at
the first battle of
Newbury on 20
September 1643.

bullets and powder and were able to answer only one shot for
three. Losses were heavy; besides Falkland the Earls of Sunder-
land and Caernarvon and many other royalists lay dead on
the field.

Essex and his victorious army, who had fought with the
courage of desperation, could not be stopped from marching
on to Reading and thence back to London. Though he had
been in the saddle all day, Rupert harassed Essex's cavalry as
they rode away to a point three miles east of Newbury, but when
the next day dawned the indomitable Roundhead musketeers
once more checked Rupert's weary troopers.

After the battle Charles ordered Rupert to garrison

Donnington Castle to the north of Newbury. Then the Prince returned with the King to Oxford. As the parliamentarians had by now evacuated Reading, it was again occupied by the royalists. Ten days later Rupert left Oxford to seize Bedford. His aim was to cut the Roundheads' communications both between London and East Anglia and between London, the east midlands and Yorkshire.

Newport Pagnell commanded a key position on these routes. Rupert put Sir Lewis Dyve, a stepbrother of George Digby, in charge there, while he himself ensured that all was well in Buckingham. The royalist dominance of the Buckingham–Newport Pagnell–Bedford area created a serious situation for the Earl of Essex, who was obliged to make a riposte. At the end of October, owing to some muddle at Oxford, for which Rupert was not responsible, Dyve was not told that fresh supplies of ammunition were on the way to him. Under pressure from Essex, therefore, he withdrew, allowing the parliamentarians to master this central position. Rupert tried to make amends by sending Dyve with a regiment of foot and a troop of horse to Towcester, three miles north of Newport Pagnell. But Dyve lost heart and asked to be allowed to return to his more comfortable governorship in Abingdon.

As has been noted, since the Queen's arrival in Oxford earlier in the year – she had set up a separate court in Merton College whence she dispatched her major-domo, Henry Jermyn, on errands of intrigue – Rupert's star had paled. Now George Digby, with whom he was at constant cross purposes, succeeded Lord Falkland as secretary of state, which did not help him at all. He still had his difficulties with Wilmot; indeed it was reported from Oxford that he was 'at a true distance with many of the officers of horse'. His principal friends were the Duke of Richmond and his beautiful wife Mary (daughter of the first Duke of Buckingham) whom Rupert is said, on good authority, to have admired. When the Prince was in Bedfordshire Richmond wrote to him to reassure him that no 'wrong judgments' were being made about him in Oxford, that he (Richmond) had assurances from the King, 'who also spoke for the Queen', while Digby had expressed his grief that Rupert was upset by 'some doubtful expressions' in his letters. Nevertheless it is clear that Rupert's influence in the councils of war had diminished.

He had to accept orders about securing Donnington, about sending part of his cavalry to Chester and about the collection of contributions of money in Berkshire. It may be that Rupert's impetuous behaviour and independence of mind created enemies unnecessarily.

Yet whatever his personal difficulties were, they did not affect his loyalty to his uncle or his energy as a commander. As Veronica Wedgwood justly observes in her book *The King's War*, in writing about the situation in the autumn of 1643: 'The tireless Prince was fortifying Towcester, recruiting in the Welsh marshes, planning the reception and distribution of the force from Ireland, organizing a ceaseless and – to Londoners – nerve-racking series of raids in the Chilterns and the Thames valley.' His one great friend, the Duke of Richmond, was sent away on a mission to Paris. He had to put up with what he regarded as insolence from other courtiers, so he spent as little time as he could in Oxford.

Indeed, it seems that Rupert at this time in his life had an almost psychopathic belief that everyone was against him, a mild persecution complex or perhaps, since he was after all a German, a sort of xenophobia. Digby and Wilmot, whatever their faults, were unquestionably loyal to the King's cause and fought bravely for him. The Queen, it is true, was at one stage jealous of Rupert's influence with her husband and dubious about the wisdom of his advice; but, as often as not, women are changeable creatures. The Queen's close friend, Lord Jermyn (who, long after Charles I's death, she was even rumoured to have married), went out of his way to pacify the Prince. Jermyn wrote him effusive letters; in March 1644 he told Rupert that he had kept 'a particular watch' on Digby and was confident that he had not failed in anything. Earlier Digby had assured Rupert of his faithfulness to his service, of his industriousness, affection and obedience, and of his prompt execution of his commands. Lord Percy, another of Rupert's *bêtes-noires*, expressed sorrow at about the same time for Rupert's displeasure over a warrant sent by the King to the storekeeper at Bristol, but added that it was not his fault and indeed had nothing to do with him. Lord Wilmot punctiliously reported to Rupert all problems relating to the cavalry.

As to the King, it is obvious that at the beginning of 1644 he regarded Rupert as his right-hand man in military affairs: for he appointed the Prince to a wide command in north-west England including Cheshire. Afterwards South Wales was added to his responsibilities and he was given the title of President of Wales. Before that he had been created Duke of Cumberland and Earl of Holderness and had sat in a parliament that met at Oxford. Finally, in April he was offered the mastership of the horse after the first Duke of Hamilton, who previously held this honorific post, had been disgraced for failing to warn the King about the dangers from Scotland.

If anything, too many honours and duties were showered upon the Prince. Everyone asked for his help. John, now Lord, Byron, who commanded at Chester, whither he had returned after suffering defeat at the hands of Sir Thomas Fairfax in the Battle of Nantwich on 26 January, wanted Rupert to take up his headquarters there. The Marquis of Newcastle, whose hold on north-eastern England was threatened when a Scots army, having agreed to join in a military alliance with the parliament at Westminster, crossed the Tweed on 19 January 1644, begged Rupert to come to his assistance. The Earl of Derby wrote pathetically to the Prince asking him to relieve Lathom House in Lancashire where his wife, a Frenchwoman, had been defying a Roundhead siege for several weeks. The King sent him a series of contradictory orders ranging from instructions to intercept a convoy in Worcestershire to orders to move down into the south-west of England.

But in fact Rupert was more or less left to his own devices during the first half of 1644. The septuagenarian general-in-chief, Lord Forth, had been sent by the King to reinforce Lord Hopton, who had moved into Hampshire. (They were defeated at the Battle of Cheriton by Waller at the end of March.) In Forth's absence the King's council of war had little military advice of value to offer; indeed Charles told Rupert that without his presence this council – 'that committee which I call yours' – could only pronounce generalized opinions.

In spite of Lord Byron's advice to the contrary, Rupert set up his headquarters at Shrewsbury; thence he moved around visiting the various garrisons which came within his extensive command. He brought off one coup at Market Drayton on 5

March, when he managed to trap a whole parliamentarian infantry regiment and take it prisoner.

A week later while he was in Chester, concerning himself with the arrival of reinforcements from Ireland, he received news that Newark was being besieged by a Roundhead force of about 7,000 men under the command of Sir John Meldrum. This was extremely dangerous to the royalists, for the loss of Newark would sever communications between Oxford and the northeast. Rupert at once rode out of Chester and approached Newark by way of Lichfield and Ashby-de-la-Zouch, picking up musketeers and other soldiers from various garrisons as he went. At two o'clock in the morning of 21 March he arrived outside Newark by moonlight and completely surprised Meldrum. Although the royalists came in to the south of the town Rupert then swept round to the north-east and occupied Beacon Hill; this hill overlooked Meldrum's artillery and infantry which were stationed in a burnt-down fortified mansion just to the north of the town and west of the river Trent, while his cavalry were massed in front of them. Rupert immediately ordered his troopers to attack; the Newark garrison sallied forth to the south-east. So Meldrum was surrounded and he surrendered on the following day.

The rejoicing in Oxford at this brilliant victory was immense. Writing from the north to congratulate Rupert, the Marquis of Newcastle said that he hoped Rupert would come to help him soon, and King Charles advised him 'to eschew Hannibal's error in not right using, as well as you imitate him in getting of, victories'. But Rupert was unable to push north from Newark because his was a makeshift army: the contingents he had collected had to be returned to their garrison duties.

The relief of Newark on 22 March was offset by the royalist defeat at Cheriton (east of Winchester in Hampshire) already noted, while the fright given to the parliamentarian army in eastern England was compensated for when that army, led by the Earl of Manchester, with Oliver Cromwell as his second-in-command, captured Lincoln at the beginning of May. Moreover, under pressure from the Scots the Marquis of Newcastle was compelled to retreat from Northumberland and shut himself up in the city of York. Here he was besieged by the Scots and a Yorkshire army under Lord Fairfax, who were joined early in June by Manchester's army.

At the beginning of April Rupert was back at his head-quarters in Shrewsbury busily recruiting. In mid-April the Queen, who was pregnant, decided to leave the danger area and go into the safer south-west: she gave birth to her last daughter at Exeter on 16 June. Rupert was ordered by her anxious husband to accompany the Queen, but Charles quickly realized how foolish it would be to dispatch his best general on such an errand and saw her off himself instead; they were never to meet again. On 25 April Rupert returned to Oxford, where he stayed for ten days pressing his advice on the King. He urged that the army which he had now collected with much difficulty should be left intact and not milked for other pur-poses. He suggested that his brother Prince Maurice should be reinforced with cavalry – Maurice had been occupied in besieg-ing the port of Lyme in Dorset since March – so as to steady the position in the south-west, and that he himself should go into Lancashire to stabilize the situation there and pick up more recruits before marching across England to the relief of the Marquis of Newcastle. Meanwhile he proposed that the King himself should act defensively, maintaining strong infantry gar-risons at Banbury, Abingdon, Reading and other strategic points around Oxford, plus a mobile reserve of cavalry so as to hamper any enemy offensive against Oxford.

In the event, after Rupert had left Shrewsbury for the north, the King and the council of war at Oxford changed their minds. No doubt that was owing to the return of Lord Forth, the King's general-in-chief, from Hampshire, for at this point Charles ack-nowledged his services by creating him Earl of Brentford. In any case Reading was abandoned on 18 May, and its garrison used to reinforce the King's army. A week later Abingdon sur-rendered, whereupon the King withdrew from Oxford into Worcestershire.

Though by abandoning these two towns and recalling troops from Gloucestershire Charles built up the forces at his disposal, he was certainly hard pressed after Rupert's departure, and if the Earl of Essex and Sir William Waller had stuck together Oxford might have fallen, the King been defeated and the war ended. Afterwards Charles apologized to Rupert for neglecting

James Stanley seventh
Earl of Derby, and
Charlotte his French
wife who courageously
defended Lathom
House in Lancashire
when it was besieged
by the Roundheads.
Rupert raised the siege
in June 1644.

his advice, saying 'I believe that if you had been with me, I had not been put to those straits I am now in.' Fortunately for the royalists, however, Essex and Waller were on bad terms. Essex decided of his own accord to march off to the west of England to relieve Lyme, while Waller's army was left outnumbered in Worcestershire.

Rupert rode out of Shrewsbury on 16 May to carry out a lightning campaign in Lancashire. He had with him some 2,000 horse and 6,000 foot. He aimed to clear Lancashire, which except for Puritan Manchester and Bolton (the latter said to

Charlotte, d. of Claud
de la Tremouille, Duc
de Thouars m 1622
James Stanley Lord
Strange of Knockyn later
7 Earl of Derby celebra-
ted for her defences of
Latham House compelled
to surrender Isle of Man.
B. 1599. D. 1664.

be 'the Geneva of the north') was reputedly royalist in sympathy. He marched through Whitchurch, Chester, where he
appointed his close friend, Will Legge, as governor, then Knuts-
ford and Stockport, where he was joined by James Stanley, Earl
of Derby, still anxious about his French wife (who had been
holding out at Lathom House, between Stockport and Bolton,
for nearly three months). Colonel Alexander Rigby, an enemy
of the Stanleys, was in charge of the siege of Lathom House
and made rather a mess of it, considering that he outnumbered
the garrison by two to one; as soon as he heard of the approach

of the noble lady's avengers, he raised the siege and withdrew to Bolton. Rupert, skirting Manchester to the west, launched three infantry regiments against the fortifications of Bolton, but its garrison beat them back and defiantly flung the body of an Irish soldier, who had been taken prisoner and hanged, over the town wall. Infuriated by this gesture, Rupert dismounted from his horse and himself led his infantry to the storm. History does not record whether Rupert summoned the garrison or not, but after a victorious assault, in which the Earl of Derby played his part, a third of the garrison was put to the sword and the captured colours were presented to the Countess of Derby, whose home was thus relieved.

Two days later Lord Goring, with 5,000 horse (some of whom the Marquis of Newcastle had let go before the siege of York began during the previous April), joined Rupert in Bury. Then the Prince returned to Bolton and marched through Wigan to Liverpool, which was already a busy port and, like Chester, a disembarkation point for troops coming from Ireland. Rupert had hoped to pick up useful supplies of food and ammunition there, but the garrison held out for four days, so he was disappointed. The town was handed over to butchery and plunder. So concerned was the Committee of Both Kingdoms in London, which was nominally in control of the parliamentarian and Scottish armies, that it dispatched Sir Henry Vane the younger to York to suggest that a detachment should be sent by its besiegers to deal with Rupert in Lancashire. However, the generals outside York decided that they would be wiser to continue with the siege, which they believed was nearing its end, and cope with Rupert when, as they fully expected, he arrived there.

Having taken the whole of Lancashire except Manchester, Rupert rested for a time in Lathom House. It has been suggested that he was angered by the news which he received from Oxford, where, he believed, his enemies were intriguing against him. But the evidence for that is slight; it is much more likely that he decided to rest the troops he had brought from Shrewsbury while he reorganized his army to accommodate not only the accession of Goring's troopers but also the levies raised by the Earl of Derby and the Irishmen he had picked up at Chester.

Furthermore, not having obtained the gunpowder which he had expected to find in Liverpool, he was compelled to send to Oxford for fresh supplies. His letters crossed dispatches for himself from Oxford; one of them was a famous letter written by Charles I from Worcestershire in which he begged his nephew to relieve York:

> If York be lost [the King wrote] I shall esteem my crown little less ... unless supported by your sudden march to me, and a miraculous conquest in the south, before the effects of their northern power can be found here. But if York be relieved, and you beat the rebels' army of both kingdoms, which are before it, then (but otherwise not) I may possibly make a shift (upon the defensive) to spin out time until you come to assist me. Wherefore I command and conjure you, by the duty and affection which I know you bear me, that, all new enterprises laid aside, you immediately march, according to your first intention with all your forces to the relief of York. But if that be either lost, or have freed themselves from the besiegers, or that, for want of powder, you cannot undertake the work, that you immediately march with your whole strength directly to Worcester to assist me and my army; without which, or your having relieved York by beating the Scots, all the successes you can afterwards have must infallibly be useless to me.

This letter, said to have been drafted by Lord Digby, was somewhat obscurely worded, especially as Charles observed in it that he had been obliged to give Rupert 'peremptory commands'. But read in the cold light of history, its significance is pretty clear, especially if it is remembered that it was written when Rupert was still campaigning in Lancashire. What Charles meant was that Rupert must now leave Lancashire and go at once to York. If by the time he got there he found either that the city was already lost or that the garrison had driven off the besiegers, then he was to come back at once to reinforce the royalists in Worcestershire. Thus Rupert was offered alternatives once he reached York. But in fact it is known that in the heat of action the Prince impetuously interpreted the letter as giving him strict orders not only to relieve York but to fight the

1 MAY — 9 DEC. 1643

- - - - - Areas controlled by the Royalists 1 May
————— Areas controlled by the Parliamentarians 1 May
▨ Areas controlled by the Royalists 9 Dec.
▦ Areas controlled by the Parliamantarians 9 Dec.
—·—·— Bdy. of the Eastern Association Sept. 1643
★ Battle of 1643

K. OF SCOTLAND

NORTH SEA

Berwick

Newburn 1640 · Newcastle ★
Carlisle · Durham
Bolton Castle
Scarborough
Ripon
Bridlington Bay
Lancaster · York
IRISH SEA
Adwalton Moor
Preston · Leeds · Hull
Lathom House · Bolton · Wakefield
Liverpool · Manchester
Anglesey · Gainsborough
Holy I. · Warrington · Sheffield · Winceby
Chester · Lincoln
Denbigh · Nantwich
The Wash
Nottingham · Boston
Hopton Heath · Castle Rising
Shrewsbury · Lichfield · Leicester · King's Lynn · Norwich
Cardigan Bay
Montgomery · Tamworth
Naseby · Eastern Association
Cardigan · Worcester · Northampton · Cambridge
Hereford · Edgehill 1642
Brecon · Colchester
Monmouth · Gloucester
Raglan Castle · Oxford · Chelmsford
Pembroke · Runsdown Hill · Chalgrove
Roundway Down · Brentford · LONDON
Bristol · Reading · Turnham Green
Bath · Newbury · Maidstone · Dover
Bideford · Langport
Bridgwater · Wardour Castle
Taunton · Arundel
Stratton · Exeter · Dorchester · Poole
Bradock Down · Portsmouth
Lostwithiel · Weymouth · I. of Wight
Dartmouth
Land's End

North Channel
Solway Firth
I. of Man
Morecambe B.
Cardigan Bay
St George's Channel
Bristol Channel
Str. of Dover
ENGLISH CHANNEL

ENGLAND AND WALES

NOV. 1644—DEC. 1645

- – – – Areas controlled by the Royalists Nov. 1644
- ——— Areas controlled by the Parliamentarians Nov. 1644
- Areas controlled by the Royalists at the end of 1645
- Areas controlled by the Parliamentarians at the end of 1645
- • Places held by the King within areas controlled by the Parliamentarians
- ★ Battle with date
  1644

K. OF SCOTLAND

NORTH SEA

Berwick

★ 1645 Philiphaugh

Newcastle

Carlisle   Durham

Bolton Castle

Scarborough

Marston Moor 1644

Bridlington Bay

Lancaster   York

Leeds   Selby   Hull

Lathom House   Sandal Castle

Anglesey   Liverpool   Stockport   Sheffield

Holy I.   Gainsborough

Caernarvon   Beeston Castle   Rowton 1645   Hulm

The Wash

Nantwich 1644   Nottingham   Newark   Castle Rising

Shrewsbury   Zouch   Belvoir Castle   King's Lynn

Ashby de la   Leicester   Norwich

Cardigan Bay   Lichfield

Naseby 1645

Cardigan   Worcester   Northampton   Huntingdon

Hereford   Tewkesbury   Bedford   Cambridge

Brecon   Banbury   Cropredy Bridge   Saffron Walden

Monmouth   Gloucester   Oxford   Colchester

Raglan Castle   Chelmsford

Pembroke   Donnington Castle

Bristol   Newbury 1644   LONDON

Bristol Channel   Bath   1645   Besing House   Maidstone   Dover

Bridgwater   Langport   Langford   Winchester

Torrington   1645   House

Taunton   Southampton   Arundel   Str. of Dover

Exeter   Portsmouth

Lostwithiel 1644   Lyme Regis   Corfe Castle   I. of Wight

Plymouth

Land's End

ENGLISH CHANNEL

DURING THE CIVIL WAR

armies that were besieging it. Charles spoke of Rupert's beating the Scots, but surely he must have known that the armies of Manchester (with Cromwell as second-in-command) and Fairfax were together nearly as large as the Scottish force. In spite of the recruiting carried out by Rupert and Goring these armies altogether outnumbered the royalists by three to two.

So Rupert moved from Lancashire into Yorkshire across the Pennines by way of Preston, Ribchester, Clitheroe, Gisburn, Skipton and Denton, reaching Knaresborough, fourteen miles west of York, on 30 June. It is perhaps a comment on Rupert's life and times, when there was one law for the rich and another for the poor, that having permitted plundering in Lancashire, when Rupert arrived at Denton Hall in Wharfedale, which had been the family seat of the Fairfaxes for a century, he slept the night there, admired the portraits of their ancestors, and left the house undisturbed.

As soon as the allied generals learned that Rupert was in Knaresborough they took steps to block his way to York. They received exaggerated reports about the number of men he had with him; they were fearful that he might, as at Newark, crush them between his relieving army and the garrison boldly sallying out of the city. Their main object, then, was to prevent a juncture between Rupert and Newcastle. Therefore, by placing their main force north-west of Long Marston (four miles west of York to the east of Marston Moor), with the river Nidd between them and the advancing enemy, they intended to prevent his approach either direct from Knaresborough across the moor or by way of Wetherby, which lay west-south-west of the city. They did not, however, send out troops to guard the road into York from the north-west by way of the suburb of Poppleton. They knew that if Rupert came by this route he would have to march his infantry twenty-two miles in a day and cross three rivers, the Ure at Borough Bridge, the Swale at Thornton Bridge, and the Yorkshire Ouse at Poppleton, and this seemed to them unthinkable.

A bridge of boats had been placed at Poppleton to facilitate contact between the army under the Earl of Manchester and the Scots army when they were both besieging York. Manchester left his regiment of dragoons to guard the crossing. This was the route by which Rupert in fact came. It is not entirely clear whether he sent some of his cavalry ahead towards Long Marston direct from Knaresborough in order to deceive the enemy; at any rate there is some evidence that he did so. Thus by speed and ingenuity he misled the Scots and their English allies as to the direction of his approach and so relieved the northern capital of England from danger of capture.

By evening of 1 July Rupert was able to dispatch General Goring with a message for the Marquis of Newcastle in York asking him to be ready at four o'clock the next morning to march against the retiring enemy. The Prince had already received a letter from Newcastle welcoming him as 'the Redeemer of the North and the Saviour of the Crown'. He courteously added that he was uncertain about the intentions of the allied armies, and 'neither can I resolve [them] since I am made of nothing but thankfulness and obedience to Your Highness'. Rupert took him at his word and assumed that he would obey his orders so long as they were couched in polite language.

In fact the allied generals had apparently decided at some time on 1 July to march away past Marston Moor towards Tadcaster to the south, with three objects in view: preventing reinforcements reaching the royalists from Cumberland and Westmorland, stopping Rupert returning to join the King, and prohibiting his movement into East Anglia where, apart from London, the chief strength of the parliamentarian army was to be found. Whether it was their deliberate intention to fight is less clear. But after Sir Thomas Fairfax, who was in charge of the cavalry rearguard, sent a message to Lord Leven, the commander of the Scots and the senior general in the three armies, that a substantial force of enemy cavalry was already deployed on Marston Moor, it was decided to recall the advance guard and main body of the infantry, which were already approaching Tadcaster, and prepare to face the enemy upon the moor. That resolution was taken at about nine o'clock on the morning of 2 July.

Rupert had only a short night's rest in the forest of Galtres north of York, for he was determined to be up early so as to arrange the coalescence of his own army with that of the relieved garrison of York. His resolution was extremely daring. His own men had marched at least twenty-two miles on the previous day – a forced march, since the average distance

William Cavendish, first Marquis of Newcastle. Although his infantry fought bravely at the battle of Marston Moor, he afterwards left the country rather than 'endure the laughter of the Court'.

moved by infantry at that time was only about ten miles a day. The York garrison had been subjected to a siege for ten weeks and was short of food, clothing and ammunition. Furthermore Rupert's force was inferior, though not grossly so, in numbers of both cavalry and infantry. No doubt he thought that the risk was worth it if he could induce his enemy to start the battle. However, it was not a practical plan. The Marquis of Newcastle did not himself meet Rupert at Long Marston until nine o'clock. Rupert greeted this magnifico with the words: 'My Lord, I wish you had come sooner with your force, but I hope we shall have a glorious day.'

76

Newcastle had in fact arrived accompanied only by his own small escort and had to tell Rupert that the rest of his men were in mutinous frame of mind, feeling that they were entitled to plunder the loot left by the besieging armies and to receive their pay and rations before they began fighting again. Newcastle had left in charge his second-in-command, the Scottish professional officer, James King, now Lord Eythin, who had fought with Rupert six years earlier at the Battle of Vlotho and had afterwards been accused of deserting him. Because of the delay Rupert gave up any idea that he might have entertained of falling upon the rear of the allies on the Tadcaster road. Instead, while waiting for Newcastle's infantry, he planned his order of battle and distributed his own troops on the moor. But his men were bored and hungry; little happened for some twelve hours except slight skirmishing and a desultory cannonade.

Although Rupert wanted a battle and told Newcastle so, he planned a defensive layout. On both his cavalry wings, the right commanded by Lord Byron and the left by Lord Goring, he interspersed platoons of musketeers among the troopers, as had been the practice of Gustavus Adolphus. As has been noticed, this meant that a cavalry offensive could not be undertaken since the musketeers could not keep up with the horsemen and might be exposed to an enemy counter-charge. In the centre he massed the infantry and behind them he placed a cavalry brigade under Sir William Blakiston that could be used to support the footsoldiers if they were in danger. Behind them again Rupert himself had a small reserve of horse at his disposal. At the front of his position, opposite the allies, who were deploying in the gently sloping Marston field, there was a long and quite deep ditch backed by hedges. This constituted an obstacle to an enemy advance, though it was less formidable to the right of the royalist line than to the left of it. However, Rupert had a regiment of dragoons on the extreme right. He placed musketeers and light guns to form a forward defensive position along the ditch, and drew up his front lines just behind the ditch. His cavalry was in three lines, his infantry in only two.

Eventually the pacified infantry from York arrived on the moor at some time in the early afternoon, led by Lord Eythin. For various reasons neither Newcastle nor Eythin wanted to fight, obviously partly because they were unsure of the morale of their men. When Rupert showed Eythin his plan of battle, the professional retorted, 'By God, sir, it is very fine on paper, but there is no such thing in the field.' When Rupert asked what was wrong with it, he was told that he had drawn up his men too near to the enemy. Rupert had clearly done this because he wanted to provoke Leven into attacking. That this was his aim is supported by a passage in the *Life of James II* (edited by J. S. Clarke in 1816 from papers left by James himself) which stated that Rupert had posted Lord Byron 'very advantageously behind a warren and a slough, with positive command not to quit his ground, but in that posture only to expect and to receive there the charge of the enemy'. Furthermore, in the skirmishing during the morning a prisoner was taken, and Rupert asked him, 'Is Cromwell there? Will they fight?' The significance of the question surely is that Cromwell's reputation as an offensive-minded cavalry leader was known to Rupert, and he hoped that Cromwell would attack at a disadvantage. In fact the parliamentarians recognized the disadvantage, but in the end they risked it.

What induced the Earl of Leven to order a battle to begin so late in the evening is not entirely clear. Presumably he had confidence in his superiority in numbers (though he may have overestimated it) and he must have hoped for surprise, which indeed he obtained, for both Rupert and Newcastle were satisfied that no major fighting would begin that day. By the time the order to advance was given it was about seven o'clock; it would be dark by nine. As Rupert went to supper both wings of the parliamentarian cavalry, Cromwell on the left, Sir Thomas Fairfax on the right, thundered down the sloping field onto the moor while real thunder and rain broke over the battlefield extinguishing the match of the musketeers in the ditch whose salvo was intended to break an enemy charge. On the royalist left, where Goring's cavalry was advantageously deployed behind a lane covered with furze bushes, it was able to cope effectively with the Yorkshire troopers; but on the right Lord Byron disobeyed Rupert's orders. Byron would have had a good chance of stopping Oliver Cromwell's assault (he led his own first line) while he was transversing the hedge and the ditch – now fast becoming a swamp in the rain – if the royalist colonel had stood his ground. Instead Byron himself advanced,

A
DOGS ELEGY,
OR
RVPERTS TEARS,

For the late Defeat given him at *Marston-moore*, neer *York*, by the Three Renowned Generalls; *Alexander Earl of Leven, Generall of the Scottish Forces*, Fardinando *Lord* Fairefax, *and the Earle of Man-chester Generalls of the English Forces in the North.*

Where his beloved Dog, named *B O Y*, was killed by a Valliant Souldier, who had skill in *Necromancy.*

Likewise the strange breed of this Shagg'd Cavalier, whelp'd of a Malignant Water-witch; With all his Tricks, and Feats.

Sad Cavaliers, *Rupert* invites you all ⟩ Close-mourners are the Witch, Pope, & devill,
That doe survive, to his Dogs Funerall. ⟩ That much lament yo'r late befallen evill.

Printed at *London*, for *G. B.* July 27. 1644.

A roundhead broadsheet, unsympathetically depicting the death of Boye at Marston Moor.

masking the fire of the musketeer platoons, and was overwhelmed by élan and numbers.

Rupert must soon have learned of the parliamentarian attack. It is unlikely that, as some historians have suggested, he at once jumped on his horse to fight Cromwell; probably, however, he heard that Goring was doing well on the left and deliberately chose to employ his reserve on the right wing. Though Byron's first line was broken, his second line was intact, so that when Rupert threw in his reserve the enemy was checked and wavered. Cromwell himself was wounded in the neck, but he headed a second charge, while his third line, mounted on Scots nags and led by the experienced Scottish officer, David Leslie, attacked Byron's flank. After this brilliant action all was in fact over. Rupert was separated from his own lifeguard and forced to hide in a bean field to escape with his life. His dog, Boye, who got loose, met his death on the battlefield.

The contest lasted only about two hours. The royalist infantry for a time fought so gallantly that the Earl of Leven and Lord Fairfax, who were both in the centre of the allied army, believing that all was lost, quitted the field, one for Leeds, the other for Hull. On the left George Goring, after driving off the Yorkshire cavalry, turned about with a view to supporting the infantry on its left flank, while Sir William Blakiston's brigade gave similar support in the centre. But Cromwell and Leslie rallied and steadied their horse, rode behind the royalist infantry still fighting courageously along the line of the ditch and attacked Goring who, as Cromwell's scoutmaster reported afterwards, 'left all thought of pursuit, and began to think that they must fight again for that victory which they thought they had already got'. After routing Goring's horse Cromwell turned upon the royalist foot. The white coats of undyed wool worn by Newcastle's infantry were stained red with blood, for they fought on until their ammunition was exhausted and even then refused to surrender. Whatever mood of mutiny they were in at the break of day, by nightfall their heroic resistance had earned them glory in defeat.

Rupert managed to cut his way out to reach York late that night. There he met Newcastle and Eythin. Eythin asked Newcastle and Rupert what they intended to do. Newcastle replied, 'I will go to Holland. I will not endure the laughter of the court.' Rupert replied shortly, 'I will rally my men.' Eythin also soon left the country. Rupert was as good as his word. He gathered together what cavalry he could, rode back into Lancashire and Cheshire and thence to Shrewsbury and to Wales, where he endeavoured to build up a new army. He did not attempt to vindicate himself for the defeat on Marston Moor. He thought that the fates had been against him, that Satan had helped his servants. Rupert had obeyed the King's orders as he understood them and had done his best to carry them out.

Chapter Five

✣

CAPTAIN-GENERAL

After the defeat on Marston Moor and before Rupert left for
the north-west he put Sir Thomas Glenham in charge of the
city of York with 3,000 men, and appointed George Goring,
who had distinguished himself in the battle, in place of the departed Marquis of Newcastle; both appointments were duly
approved by the King. But Glenham surrendered on 16 July
and the greater part of Yorkshire was lost to the Cavaliers. The
situation was little better in Lancashire, where the local royalists were twice defeated and the port of Liverpool was regained
by the parliamentarians. On the day after the battle Rupert
met Montrose for the second and last time. The Prince was in
no position to give the Marquis the assistance for which he
asked; indeed Montrose let Rupert have recruits he had collected in Cumberland and Westmorland to help replace his
losses. Rupert and Montrose were both dedicated to the King's
service and it was a fine example of unselfish cooperation.

With two such champions Charles I refused to be
despondent. Accompanied by his secretary of state, George
Digby, the King himself surprisingly defeated Sir William Waller, the ablest of the Roundhead generals, at the Battle of Cropredy Bridge north of Banbury. Furthermore, the first reports
that were received from Yorkshire were cheering. It was decided that whether Rupert was victorious or not, the King
would lead his army westwards to link up with that of Prince
Maurice. By drawing forces out of Bristol and Wales they might
hope together to outnumber the Earl of Essex, who was then
on his way to Lyme.

On 17 July Digby wrote to Rupert: 'Although there is no
matter for congratulation in the battle in the north, since the

success was not answerable to your Highness's virtue; yet it is a matter of comfort in that . . . the event was no worse, but that you have done the work you came for, of relieving York; your Highness yet remains in a condition to renew the dispute upon terms not unhopeful.' Digby did not of course know at the time he wrote that York had surrendered. What Rupert, who was habitually suspicious of Digby's honesty, thought of the letter is not recorded, but may be imagined.

While Charles was campaigning in the west, he decided to arrange what today would be called a cabinet reshuffle. Lord Wilmot, doubtfully suspected of intriguing with the enemy, was deprived of his command as lieutenant-general of the horse and put under arrest, being replaced by the ubiquitous Lord Goring, whose appointment was recommended by Rupert; Lord Percy, the master of the ordnance, was succeeded by Lord Hopton, one of the best of the royalist generals with a number of victories to his credit; and Rupert was informed that as soon as the King 'shall find means to satisfy the old general', that is to say the Earl of Brentford, who was deaf, gouty and alcoholic (but by no standard incompetent), the Prince was to be appointed 'generalissimo'. Though Rupert disliked both Wilmot and Percy, he was himself not an intriguer and had nothing to do with these changes. At the end of August Charles wrote to assure him: 'I must profess to you upon the faith of a Christian . . . that concerning your generosity and particular fidelity and friendship to me, I have implicit faith in you.' He also begged him to try to get along better with Digby, whom the King regarded as 'a faithful servant'. It was not, however, until 6 November that Brentford was gently removed and Rupert took over as general-in-chief or captain-general in his place.

Three days after Charles wrote to Rupert reaffirming his confidence in him, the King himself won a spectacular victory over the Earl of Essex at Lostwithiel in Cornwall. Charles had gathered together an effective army in the south-west to trap Essex between the southern Cornish hills and the sea. If sleeping musketeers had not allowed the Roundhead cavalry to break out at three o'clock in the morning, the victory would have been complete; as it was, the infantry surrendered on 2 September and, having been disarmed, were decimated by starvation as they tramped away.

George Goring, who succeeded Lord Wilmot as lieutenant-general of the horse on Rupert's recommendation.

But Waller, with another army, largely consisting of cavalry, was available to bar the King's difficult path back to Oxford; the Earl of Manchester had a first-class army which was summoned from East Anglia; and in the north, after the victory at Marston Moor, Parliament's Scottish allies had besieged Newcastle upon Tyne, which eventually surrendered on 19 October. Furthermore, nearly the whole of Lancashire was lost to the royalists by the late autumn, as was also Montgomery Castle in Wales. So when Rupert met the King again in Dorset at the end of September, they had to take the decision to act defensively, contracting commitments and concentrating nearly all available resources in Wales, Oxfordshire and south-west England. It was arranged that Charles's victorious army from Cornwall, which was suffering from medical casualties and scarcity of food, should be reinforced with the remains of the northern armies, while Rupert himself should go back to Bristol to strengthen its garrison and fortifications and bring assistance to the King in Wiltshire.

Rupert reached Bristol on 6 October and remained there for over three weeks. In spite of the King's assurances and the promise of the chief command, Rupert still felt that he was not altogether trusted. From Bristol he wrote to his friend, Will Legge, who was then in Chester, that 'great factions were breed-ing against him ... he being, as they report, the only cause of war in this kingdom'. Though Digby told Rupert, with reference to the generalship, that he was delighted that the army should soon be 'animated by his spirit', the Prince dis-trusted such effusive professions of admiration. It was on account of this passing mood that Rupert lingered in Bristol so long. 'Prince Rupert', wrote one who was there at the time, 'is so much governed by his ease and pleasure that everyone is disheartened that sees it.' On 11 October Charles wrote to him warning him that Basing House and the castles of Banbury and Donnington were all in danger of surrendering, while Rupert also received discouraging letters about the state of Oxford and Chester. Charles asked Rupert to meet him at Salisbury with what strength of horse and foot he could gather together and two demi-cannon; some of his men, the King said, were un-armed and needed muskets to be sent to them from Bristol. Rupert contented himself with offering advice. He was, after all, at last the King's official military counsellor, his appointment having been officially announced on 1 November. For though the boy Prince of Wales was named 'generalissimo', Prince Rupert was appointed lieutenant-general of all the King's armies, replacing the Earl of Brentford who, presumably in a fit of alcoholic euphoria, fell off his horse and broke his shoulder.

Acting in his new capacity, Rupert urged Charles not to pursue the rebels towards London if he managed to chase them away from Basing House in Hampshire, while he promised that

Whytchurche. 20. Oct. 1644.

Nepueu! I am not halfe so trubled, with Sr John Winters ill lucke, as I am glad you will be able, so soone, to March from Bristol; & that you will bring more Foote with you, then (at your being last with me) you promised: As for the reasons of my quicke Marching this way, I refer you to Digbyes relation by wch you will perceaue, there was great necessity for it, & as hitherto God hath blessed vs with successe, so I am confident you will see more & more reason for what I haue done, & that I hazarded more, if I had not hazarded as I did: So hoping to see you shortly I rest

Your louing Oncle & most faithfull frend
Charles R

A letter dated 20 October 1644 from Charles to his nephew reflects the fragility of their agreement on matters of strategy.

he himself would secure Banbury. Evidently the royalists were now baffled as to their enemy's intentions. On 20 October Rupert was told that the parliamentarian soldiers were widely dispersed, some going towards Basing and others towards Banbury. Charles naturally thought that Rupert ought now to join him from Bristol to assist him in pushing aside the enemy forces gathering in Hampshire and Berkshire and ensure his safe return to Oxford. But he was careful, as Digby explained to

Rupert, to send 'no peremptory orders'. Even when, in the last week of October, Charles encountered at Newbury the parliamentarian armies, consisting of Manchester's intact forces from East Anglia, Waller's new army, and the remnants of Essex's cavalry, Digby reiterated to Rupert that 'His Majesty sends no peremptory order'. But he did add that if Rupert could advance at once with a considerable force, the King would try to hold off the enemy from the position that he had taken up between Donnington Castle and the river Kennet to the north of Newbury town.

It may well be that after the disaster at Marston Moor the King was shy about giving 'peremptory orders' to his nephew, while Rupert may still have been sulking. In any case, he did not reach the King until after the Second Battle of Newbury. In that battle, fought on 27 October, the royalists were outnumbered but by no means disgraced. An experiment adopted by the parliamentarians of having no commander-in-chief but instead appointing a committee to direct operations was not a success. The Earl of Manchester, whose troops immediately faced the King, while Waller and Cromwell made a long detour to attack the royalists from the rear, failed to synchronize his assault with that of his colleagues. Thus they were unable to prevent the King escaping to Bath and eventually back to his base at Oxford. Rupert met the King at Bath. Together they returned to Donnington Castle, which contained a valuable train of artillery that the parliamentarians thus failed to capture. The relief of the castle is sometimes described as the Third Battle of Newbury, but it was so late in the season that neither side really wanted to resume the fight.

Rupert had now taken over in effect as commander-in-chief of the King's armies. He was also at last appointed master of the horse in Hamilton's place. Oddly enough, he seems to have resented not also being made captain of the king's lifeguard, and he actually threatened to throw up his command on this issue; but, presumably in view of the grave military situation, he dropped that piece of childishness. Indeed he could hardly have assumed the command at a less propitious moment. Sir Jacob Astley wrote to him complaining about lack of supplies and troops at Cirencester; Colonel Lisle, stationed at Farringdon, seven miles south-west of Oxford, said that the garrison

Sir Thomas Fairfax,
commander-in-chief of
the New Model Army.

was faced with famine, having eaten all the available cattle;
Sir Edward Nicholas wrote of the uncomfortable situation in
Oxford because the rebels were still in nearby Abingdon. Criti-
cal news arrived even from the west, where the siege of Taun-
ton, undertaken when Charles left Somerset, had to be aban-
doned. The only favourable tidings to reach him came from
Gloucestershire and Monmouthshire where Colonel Sir John
Wintour had thrust a party of rebels away from Chepstow
Castle. Rupert himself had a setback when, in attempting to
clear the Roundhead skirmishers away from the vicinity of
Oxford, he tried to surprise Abingdon but was disappointed.

The year 1645 opened with both sides feeling dubious about
their military prospects. The parliamentarians were shocked by
the defeat of their commander-in-chief at the Battle of Lostwithiel, following the failure of Sir William Waller at Cropredy
Bridge, and by the inability of all their generals to crush the
King at Newbury. They also had doubts about the indecisive-
ness of the Earl of Manchester; his first lieutenant, Oliver
Cromwell, accused him of an unwillingness to fight the royalists
to the finish. That was why, after considerable political

Armour worn by
cavalrymen in the New
Model Army.

manoeuvring, the two Houses at Westminster agreed in the
spring to form a fresh army, to be known as the New Model
Army, under the command of Sir Thomas Fairfax, who was
not a member of either House of Parliament, and to accept the
resignations of the Earls of Essex and Manchester from their
commands.

On the royalist side the King continued to be optimistic, but the facts were grim: except for the castles at Scarborough and Pontefract, the whole of the north-east had been lost, while the north-west was in little better shape, though Chester was still intact; in the midlands Shrewsbury surrendered to the parliamentarians in February, while in the south-west Taunton still held out defiantly under the able Colonel Robert Blake and the port of Weymouth twice changed hands, but in the end, like Plymouth, came into the control of Parliament.

In view of the general military situation, Rupert initially urged his uncle to make peace. But the terms offered to the King by Parliament during the negotiations which went on at Uxbridge for nearly a month were as stiff as they had been before the defeat of Essex. Therefore Rupert concentrated his attention on building up a new army for the King, centring his efforts upon the area around Hereford and Bristol. Charles himself nursed hopes of help from Ireland and Scotland. The Marquis of Ormonde had been ordered to come to terms with the Irish rebels so that soldiers could be released for the King's service in England, while in Scotland the Marquis of Montrose had begun his astounding campaigns with meagre resources against the covenanters – campaigns which had already forced the Earl of Leven to send back some of the troops that he had with him in England to assist his harassed fellow countrymen.

Rupert's immediate difficulties were with his own side. George Goring, who had replaced Lord Wilmot as lieutenant-general of the horse, sought and was granted an independent command by the King. On 22 January he wrote to Rupert saying that one reason why he had asked for this was that 'I found all my requests denied by your hand, and therefore desired my orders from another'. It may be remembered that before the Battle of Edgehill Rupert himself had set the precedent for the general of horse being independent of the commander-in-chief, so he was hardly in a position to complain. But it was a nasty letter. Rupert was a strong man and before the campaigning season opened he had, by insisting on his own supremacy as the King's captain-general, re-established his authority over Goring, who then proceeded to write him effusive letters. Secondly, his brother Maurice, who had replaced him in effect though not in name as President of Wales, started asking for wider powers. Lastly the King insisted on sending his fourteen-year-old son

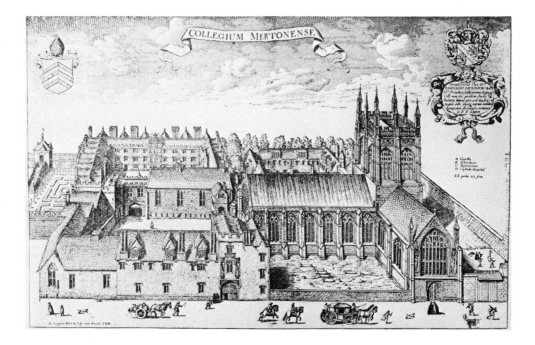

COLLEGIUM MERTONENSE

Merton College, Oxford.

Charles, Prince of Wales, to Bristol as commander-in-chief in the west with an independent court, military adviser, council of state and full powers. Naturally Rupert resented this large diminution of his authority in the very area where royalism was strongest. In mid-March he declared: 'I expect nothing but ill from the west.' Goring refused to take orders from the Prince of Wales's council, so Rupert had to go to Bristol to clear up the trouble. But Goring sulked and went off to Bath to improve his health, if not his temper. Before Rupert saw the youthful Charles he confided to his friend Will Legge, 'I now intend for Bristol to rob them [the garrison] of their arms and (if I had the power) of Prince Charles.'

In spite of these personal problems Rupert managed to restore order in Wales and along the Welsh border, though at one time he was afraid that the whole of Wales would be in rebellion if unrest were not speedily repressed. He relieved Beeston Castle near Ludlow; a rising at Hereford had to be put down; a parliamentarian force was defeated at Ledbury, seventeen miles north-west of Gloucester. By the time the campaigning season began fully in the spring of 1645 the Prince had collected both men and arms for his master. Meanwhile the Committee of Both Kingdoms ordered General Fairfax and his New Model Army to relieve Taunton, again being besieged by the royalists, while Cromwell was sent off to raid Oxford. He at once made his presence felt by routing a contingent of royalist soldiers at Islip and by capturing Bletchington House north of Islip, for which the governor was condemned to death and shot outside Merton College. Charles at once ordered Rupert back so as 'to frame our body of an army hereabouts without which not only the King's conjunction with you will be impossible, and then Prince Rupert will be forced to march hither to relieve him upon worse terms than now'.

Rupert and Maurice reached Oxford on 4 May and then withdrew by way of Woodstock to Stow-on-the-Wold, Rupert leaving Will Legge as military commander in Oxford. At Stow-on-the-Wold the King reviewed an army of 11,000 men and held a council of war. The question to be decided was whether the army should follow Fairfax to the south-west, as in the previous year the Earl of Essex had been followed, or whether the King should lead it north, to fight the weakened Scottish army (which was now at Ripon in Yorkshire) before joining Montrose. Rupert favoured the second scheme, but Charles resolved upon a compromise. Goring, with much of the cavalry, was dispatched to Taunton to resume the siege which he had re-opened in March, while Rupert collected artillery and wagons preparatory to moving north. It was a highly unsatisfactory solution which can scarcely have had Rupert's approval. In fact Taunton was relieved two days after Goring left the midlands; while Goring was on his way Fairfax was already marching back towards Oxford.

The renewed threat to Oxford, which was reported to be short of food and ammunition, obliged the King and Rupert to reconsider their strategy. They decided that they would continue their move northwards unless the situation at Oxford became desperate. As a precaution Goring, who had previously been intended to rejoin them from the south-west, was instructed to lend his help to the Oxford garrison. Legge was therefore ordered to hold out as long as he could, Goring was recalled, and the King's army advanced north across the midlands to Leicestershire where it was expected to be reinforced from Wales. While the King and his council waited upon events, an attack on the wealthy capital of the county, which Rupert had been reproved for threatening at the outset of the war, was undertaken. Leicester was quickly surrounded, Rupert himself placing the batteries. A breach was blown in the walls, but the garrison defended the breach so that an assault had to be carried out, the Cavaliers crossing the moat and scaling the city walls. The town was put to the sack and two or three hundred men and women slain. Rupert was fully entitled in view of the defence of the breach to put the entire garrison to the sword, as Cromwell was to do later at Drogheda; instead some 1,200 soldiers were taken as prisoners.

After the fall of Leicester on 31 May King Charles again changed his mind about the move farther north. During the period between the middle of May and the first week of June both sides were enveloped in a fog of war. Fairfax had no clear idea where the King was going after he left Oxford for the midlands; Charles did not appreciate the gravity of the threat to Oxford, which was now being besieged by Fairfax instead of Cromwell – Cromwell had been sent home lest the royalists intended to invade the eastern counties. For several days after the surrender of Leicester the King hesitated. Should he return to Oxford and challenge Fairfax, whose New Model Army the royalists treated with contempt, or should he press on north? Rupert still strongly favoured the march north, but he was over-ruled. Charles was in a cheerful mood. He wrote to the Queen at this time: 'I may without being too sanguine affirm that since this rebellion my affairs were never in so hopeful a way.' He had received news of Montrose's victories in Scotland and was pleased by the rapid fall of Leicester. But his advisers other than Rupert were worried about their womenfolk in Oxford and pressed the King to return there. So there was order, counter-order and disorder.

From Leicester the royalist army moved back in a leisurely manner to Daventry, roughly halfway between Leicester and Oxford. Charles put up at the Wheatsheaf Inn and went hunting. Fairfax, for his part, was on the alert. Given full authority, he broke up on 5 June from Oxford (which in any case he could not have stormed because he lacked adequate artillery to make a breach) and moved out in search of the royal army. By 12 June Fairfax had reached a point eight miles from Daventry, while the royalists, having heard that Oxford was safe after all, had again turned north. On the night of 13 June they were encamped around Market Harborough, eighteen miles north-east of Daventry, though Charles himself slept at nearby Lubenham. Rupert had left some troopers as a rear outpost at the village of Naseby, and they were caught and slaughtered in the village inn by Fairfax's advance guard. As soon as the King heard the news, he went to Market Harborough to arouse Rupert and a hasty council of war was called at midnight. Rupert has been accused of being careless and over-confident and underestimating his enemy. But he had never wanted to return south from Leicester. He wrote to his friend Legge from Daventry on 8 June that 'there was a plot to send the King [back] to Oxford, but it is undone'. He did not participate in Digby's enthusiasm for challenging Fairfax to battle with inferior numbers. Even at the midnight council of war on 13 June he counselled retreat, at least until reinforcements, which were available, could reach them. But it was too late. The King ordered Rupert to prepare for battle.

The Battle of Naseby, then, was fought against Rupert's wishes. He had to make the best of things, but the difficulties were severe. Both in cavalry and infantry he was numerically inferior to Fairfax and Cromwell, though how much inferior is uncertain. A garrison had been left at Leicester, but, to set against that, part of the garrison from Newark had joined the main army. Goring had refused, or at any rate been unable, to return from the west, as he had been ordered to do. His seasoned cavalry might have made all the difference. The infantry had marched about twenty miles the day before, while the 2,000 Yorkshire troopers, the remnants of Newcastle's army, were demoralized and even mutinous because they had been hoping to go home and were displeased at being brought south from Leicester.

It is as difficult to interpret the complicated manoeuvring before the battle began as it is to ascertain the numbers that fought on each side. After the decision had been taken in the middle of the night that the royalists must face a battle next day, Rupert drew them up some time before eight o'clock on

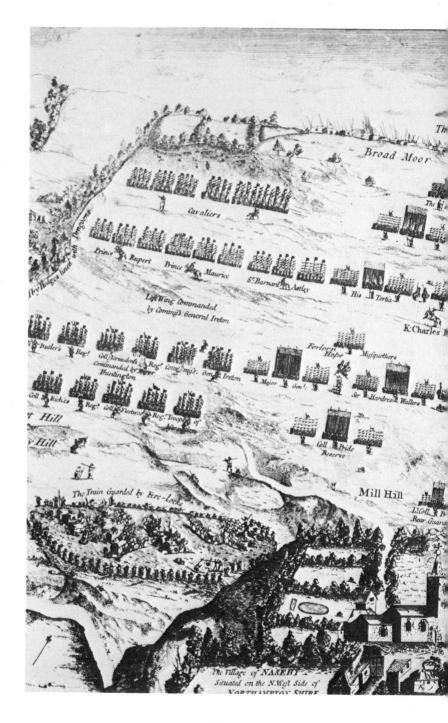

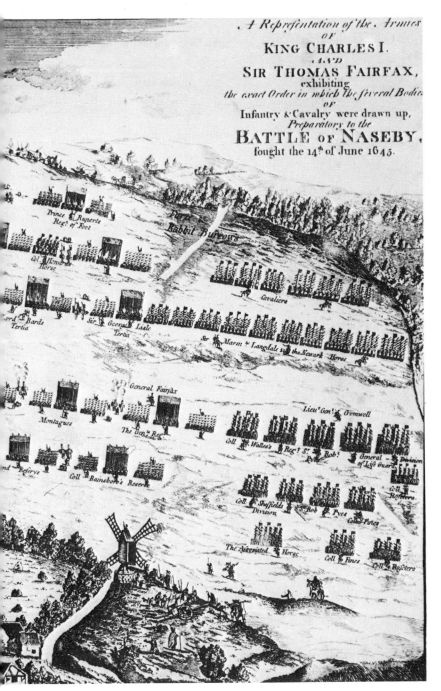

The Battle of Naseby,
14 June 1645.

a diagonal line two miles south of Market Harborough between
the villages of East Farndon and Great Oxenden, which constituted a defensible ridge. He then personally reconnoitred the
enemy's position and was surprised to detect a movement to
its left. The movement that he saw may have been a change
of position to avoid some boggy ground; it may have been a
slight withdrawal behind one of the numerous ridges; or it may
simply have been a rival reconnoitring party. At any rate
Rupert then decided to move his own army forward and to the
right on a slight eminence called Dust Hill. Fairfax was also
ensconced on two hills, Red Hill and Mill Hill; between the
two armies was an expanse of heath known as Broad Moor.
Both armies were deployed with the cavalry on the wings and
the infantry in the centre. But each position had a novel feature.
In the Roundhead army Cromwell had instructed Colonel
John Okey, with a regiment of dragoons, to line a row of hedges
on the extreme left of the parliamentarian army from which
an advancing cavalry attack could be enfiladed by carbiniers.
In the King's army the infantry was supported by five cavalry
divisions, say some 800 troopers. In the rear the King, who
was himself in supreme command, had a reserve of one
infantry regiment, his lifeguard of foot and his cavalry lifeguard.

The battle began about ten o'clock with Rupert and his
brother Maurice charging the left wing of the parliamentarian
horse commanded by Commissary-General Henry Ireton, who
had been promoted to that post the day before. Rupert's charge
was described by enemy chroniclers as made resolutely 'with
undaunted courage' and 'with such gallantry as few ever saw
the like'. Evidently Rupert had decided that the best chance
of winning the battle was to attack at all costs, even though
he had fewer men and had to advance uphill. Ireton made the
mistake of trying to turn upon the flank of the royalist infantry
after Rupert had swept past him, which caused him to be badly
wounded and taken prisoner. The royalist footsoldiers also
fought splendidly under Lord Astley. It may well be that the
error at Edgehill was repeated, that is to say that Rupert
believed the battle had been won before the enemy cavalry on
the opposite wing to his own had been put out of action. In
fact Lieutenant-General Cromwell, who was in charge of the
parliamentarian right, quickly routed the Yorkshire cavalry

before turning his horse to attack the royalist infantry on his left. While Rupert and his troopers thrust on to Naseby, Colonel Okey ordered his dragoons, lining the hedges, who had been unable to halt Rupert's offensive, to mount their nags so as to attack the royalist infantry on their front. Thus the royalist foot-soldiers, who had been fighting bravely at push of pike and butt of musket, were crushed.

The King had hesitated or allowed himself to be deflected at the crucial moment when he might have thrown in his life-guard under Lord Lichfield to reinforce the cavalry divisions which Rupert had placed to stiffen the infantry. Perhaps Rupert reflected ironically that if he had commanded the life-guard, as he had wanted to do, it might have been used more effectively. At any rate the royalists were unable to counter-attack. After their defeat Charles and the two German princes managed to get away first to Leicester and then to Ashby-de-la-Zouch; but no fewer than 5,000 of their officers and men surrendered on the field of battle, which suggests complete demoralization.

How far was Rupert to blame for the defeat? The Prince realized that 'the fault of it' would be 'put upon him': that was natural enough; he was after all captain-general. What his critics, led by Digby, claimed was that he did not obtain sufficient evidence about the strength and dispositions of Fairfax's army, that he had no council of war to decide how his own army would best be deployed, and did not even follow the advice of Lord Astley, who was in charge of the infantry; and finally that he had no adequate reserve. But none of these accusations had much foundation. It was the King who decided upon challenging Fairfax to battle and the King who commanded the reserve. As Digby knew and admitted, the reason why Rupert was angry with him was not so much because of his intrigues and 'obscure' and 'oblique' reflections on the Prince's military competence as because he had pressed Charles to return to Oxford through Daventry instead of moving north from Market Harborough. Once that decision had been taken, it would no doubt have been difficult to avoid fighting a battle, though Rupert appears to have believed that they could have done so. Moreover, the idea that Legge could not have held out against Fairfax for several weeks, when Oxford had previously resisted the parliamentarian generals for years, is not substantiated.

Nine days after the battle a council of war was held at Hereford, which Rupert and the King had reached by a circuitous route through the west midlands. They had little choice about their next moves. They would have to recruit a new army in the west and concentrate their defence upon Somerset, Devonshire, Cornwall, Worcester, Hereford, South Wales and Bristol. Messages were sent to Goring to try to build up his forces in Somerset, while Rupert visited the Prince of Wales and his counsellors, who had moved from Bristol to Barnstaple in north Devon. The trouble was that the Prince of Wales's military adviser, Lord Hopton, did not get on with Goring any better than Rupert did with Digby. As Sir Edward Hyde, who was a member of the Prince of Wales's council, wrote to Rupert: 'For God's sake, sire, prevent accidents that may make us less at unity among ourselves, and then I am confident the enemy will not prevail.' Furthermore the King himself, who spent three weeks in some comfort at Ragland Castle south-west of Hereford, showed no true leadership. At the beginning of July he told Rupert and Goring that they must do what they thought best, while he himself was unable to decide whether to join Rupert in Bristol, go over to Ireland or make a dash for Scotland, where Montrose was still victorious. Rupert wanted Charles to come to Bristol because he thought he would never reach Scotland safely and that the Irish would fail him. The King at first seriously considered going to Bristol, but immediately changed his mind and played with the idea of leading a select cavalry force north into Scotland.

By then the royalist situation was rapidly deteriorating everywhere. Goring was defeated by Fairfax at the Battle of Langport on 10 July and abandoned his base at Bridgwater. Rupert had to yield Bath to the enemy. Fairfax next prepared to besiege Bristol, while the Scots eventually arrived from the north to attack Hereford. But King Charles now roused himself from his torpor to good purpose. The Earl of Leven had been compelled by Montrose's victories to send nearly all his horse back to Scotland, and by the skilful use of such cavalry as he had the King forced Leven to raise the siege of Hereford, which he was able to enter on 4 September.

On that very same day Fairfax, who had been blockading Bristol for a fortnight, summoned Rupert to surrender, pleading with him that further bloodshed would serve no useful purpose and arguing that the King's crown was not in peril: 'We fight to maintain it there.' Since only a few weeks earlier Rupert had written from Bristol to his friends in Oxford that the King had 'no way left to preserve his posterity, kingdom and nobility but by a treaty' and therefore that it was 'a more prudent way to retain something than to lose all', Fairfax was in a sense pushing against an open door. Yet Rupert was firmly told by Charles that even though he faced ruin he would go on fighting to the last.

Rupert had done everything he could to strengthen Bristol by fortifying it with over a hundred guns and collecting sufficient supplies of food to sustain a long siege, but once Fairfax resolved to storm the city the Prince realized that his position was hopeless. He had, he said, only 1,500 effective professional soldiers against Fairfax's army of 12,000. There was plague in the town and the citizens, including the militia, were demoralized and apathetic. Rupert had not sufficient troops to man the five miles of wall any more than Nathaniel Fiennes had when Rupert himself attacked Bristol in 1643. The Prince's council of war was of the opinion that though they might resist a first assault, they would have to succumb to a second. Nor did they believe that any relief was in prospect.

On the north-east side of the town the Roundheads broke through on 10 September, slaughtering the entire garrison of one of the strongest forts in the city because it had refused to accept quarter when summoned. Consideration was given to the possibility of Rupert and the rest of the garrison retreating into the castle for a last stand, or even of Rupert himself forcing his way out with his cavalry, leaving the castle and citadel to be defended by infantry. But it was decided that the first course was hopeless, as the 'great fort' or citadel lacked an adequate water supply, while the second course would have been dishonourable. On 11 September Fairfax accepted surrender on generous terms. Rupert himself was allowed to leave for Oxford. As soon as the King heard the news, he dismissed his nephew from all his military offices.

Chapter Six

✤

RUPERT

AS A

SOLDIER

Rupert's career as an active military commander-in-chief closed when he was barely twenty-six years old, and it ended on a sour note. Was Charles I justified in thinking that his nephew had surrendered Bristol precipitately? The King's point of view is understandable. He himself had just successfully relieved Hereford from siege by the Scots; he had given Rupert a completely free hand; Rupert had been in Bristol since the beginning of July, and admittedly he had obtained enough food to stand a blockade for six months or more. If Oliver Cromwell's figures, given to Parliament after the town's surrender on 11 September, are to be trusted, the Prince had 140 cannon, 2,500 infantry, 1,000 cavalry and some 1,500 trained bands and auxiliaries. Cromwell was not a liar, but in the moment of triumph victors are liable to exaggerate (as the Royal Air Force did after the Battle of Britain in 1940). Probably the truth lay somewhere between the figures Rupert gave of 100 cannon and 1,500 effectives and those that Cromwell recorded in his dispatch.

Charles took the view that if Rupert had held out in Fort Royal, or 'the great fort', and the medieval castle – which was protected by a moat, a massive keep and a parapet wall – for another two or three weeks, he could have been relieved either by Goring's army or by the King's own army, neither of which was very far distant. As Rupert had told the King on 12 August that the town could hold out for four months unless there were a mutiny, Charles naturally felt angry.

But it has to be remembered that the King then had only some 2,000 men at his disposal, while Goring after his defeat at Langport had at most 5,000. A parliamentarian newsletter published on 12 September, the day after the surrender, stated

A curious portrait of Prince Rupert. The name
'Cuyp' appears in the upper right-hand corner.

that Goring was 'still about Exeter, more inclined to drink and plunder than to relieve Bristol'. Indeed Fairfax had intercepted a letter from Goring saying that he could not possibly get to Bristol for three weeks. That was one of the things which decided Fairfax in favour of a storm. The estimated size of the royalist forces available for relief was at most some 7,000 men, compared with at least 12,000 commanded by Fairfax and Cromwell. They had sufficient soldiers and artillery to surround the entire city.

Rupert claimed that he had shown industry and integrity since his return to Bristol in July, but that he had been obliged to post some of his men and guns in outlying garrisons. He had brought in cattle and corn from the neighbourhood of Wales; and no doubt he might have argued that when he told the King that Bristol could hold out for four months, it was on the assumption of a blockade and not a storm. After all, Colonel Fiennes, with about the same sized garrison, had been obliged to surrender to assault by Rupert in 1643. Fairfax had launched his main attacks from precisely the same directions that Rupert had chosen, that is to say from the north-east, where the capture of Prior Hill's fort after three hours' fighting caused a breach in the town's defences, and from the south-east, where resistance by the garrison was firm. Was it possible after all this that Rupert could have carried on the fight from the medieval castle or citadel? As has been noted, the water supply would not have lasted more than a few days. Moreover, to prolong the fighting would have been extremely hard on the garrison (though, after all, soldiers sometimes have to fight on with little hope) and on the inhabitants of the city and the port who were already afflicted with plague and menaced from the sea. It was really only a practical proposition to fight on until the last man and the last round if relief could be speedily expected.

Rupert complained not unjustly that he had received neither positive orders nor up-to-date intelligence. On 24 July the King had assured Rupert of his 'affection' and 'confidence' and had at the same time taken away some of his arms and powder. When Rupert had advised him to treat for peace, Charles had answered that speaking as a mere soldier or statesman 'There is no probability but that of my ruin', and insisted that he must resist to the last in defence 'of his religion, crown and friends'.

Sir Edward Nicholas, one of Charles's secretaries of
state, was given the task of handing Rupert his
discharge.

A contemporary impression of Rupert's brother, Maurice. At his birth his mother is reputed to have said, 'He had better be a soldier.'

A week later Charles told his nephew that although he did not know how Bristol would do without him, he could wish he was with the Prince of Wales, who was then in Devonshire; but he left the decision entirely to Rupert. After that, according to the Prince himself, 'during the whole of the siege' he 'never received any intelligence' either from the King or from Goring, though he himself wrote ten letters to Oxford during that period. Hence he could not measure how events were shaping elsewhere and

104

whether relief was likely or a treaty of peace under consideration. Finally, it was not Rupert alone who took the decision
to surrender on honourable terms but the whole of his council
of war, which contained several brave and loyal officers.

Rupert reached Oxford on 11 September only to find that
the King was not there but had sent instructions that Sir
Edward Nicholas, one of his secretaries of state, should give
Rupert his discharge and a pass to go abroad and that he should
place Rupert's friend Legge, the governor of Oxford, under
arrest. Nicholas reluctantly obeyed these orders and reported
back that Rupert had 'not £50 in all the world and could not
feed himself nor his servants'. Charles also wrote to Prince
Maurice, who was sick with the plague at Worcester, telling
him of his brother's dismissal for 'his unhandsome quitting the
castle and fort of Bristol', but begging Maurice himself to continue in his command. It was ironical that at about the same
time that Bristol was under siege the eldest surviving brother
of Rupert and Maurice, Charles Louis, now the Elector Palatine in name if not in fact, was being entertained in Whitehall
and promised a pension of £8,000 a year by Parliament. And
there were plenty of wagging tongues, led by the exiled Queen
Henrietta Maria, to suggest that, knowing that his eldest
brother was in the good books of Parliament, Rupert had trea-
sonably betrayed the city he had been ordered to defend. On
the other hand, Colonel John Butler, the Roundhead officer
assigned by Fairfax to conduct Rupert to Oxford, asserted on
his word of honour that Rupert could not have held Bristol
without more men. What Prince Maurice thought was revealed
when he left his sick-bed in Worcester to join Rupert at Banbury.

Rupert was determined to establish his innocence and to
wipe away the blot on his escutcheon. As soon as he returned
to Oxford, he wrote a long letter to the King asking permission
to see him so that he could put his case to him. When Charles
had heard of the loss of Bristol he had left Wales and, after
wandering round the midlands, reached Newark, which was
still occupied by the royalists. Having met his brother in Banbury Rupert resolved to go to Newark; this meant fighting their
way past a number of parliamentarian posts and garrisons.
Besides Maurice and a number of noble friends, including Lord

Hawley, who had been at Bristol, Rupert had managed to retain a troop of horse. His party succeeded in getting through Northampton, but was then confronted by the governor of Burghley House near Stamford, which Cromwell had captured in July 1643. The governor actually shot at Rupert with his pistol, but missed, and the Prince shot him dead. While making for Belvoir Castle in Lincolnshire, which was still friendly, he was intercepted by a contingent of parliamentarian cavalry, outnumbering his own party by three to one. Rupert twice charged them and beat them off; when Roundhead reinforcements arrived the Prince cried: 'We have beaten them twice, we must beat them once more, and then over the pass and away!' Though several of his troopers were killed in these skirmishes, Rupert reached Belvoir in safety before riding on to Newark. The Prince ignored the prohibition from his uncle against coming to see him and was greeted outside the town by the governor, Sir Richard Willys, a friend of his, who allowed him to meet the King. When Rupert told Charles that he had come to give an account of the loss of Bristol, the King ignored him and went to supper. Rupert and Maurice followed him. Then the King yielded to their pleading, and a court martial was ordered for the following day.

The court martial, or council of war, as it was called, met on 18 and 21 October. After these two hearings the King declared that Rupert had been guilty neither of cowardice nor of infidelity, but still asserted that his nephew should have kept the castle and the citadel longer since he himself was ready to come to the relief. He was in fact tempering a verdict of guilty with faint praise. Charles then made matters worse for Rupert by kicking Willys upstairs, making him captain of the royal lifeguard and replacing him as governor of Newark by Lord Bellasyse, a friend of Lord Digby. Digby, when he heard that Rupert, of whom he had always been jealous, was coming to Newark, had asked permission from the King to lead a regiment north in an attempt to join Montrose in Scotland. He did not in fact get to him but fled the country. It was Digby who had persuaded Charles to dismiss Legge from his post at Oxford on the totally false ground that he was in communication with the enemy. Charles's judgement and behaviour were at fault. But Rupert did not improve matters when he and some of his friends

Opposite A portrait of a grave Charles I.

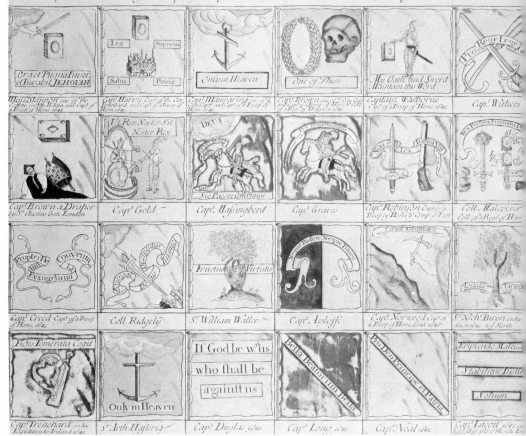

'THE DEVISES
MOTTOS &c used by
the Parliament Officers
on STANDARD
BANNERS, &c in the
late CIVIL WARS',
from an eighteenth-
century edition of the
Earl of Clarendon's
*History of the Great
Rebellion.*

pushed their way into the King's presence while he was having
dinner to protest about Willys's dismissal from the governorship
and to condemn the absent Digby and, by implication, the King
for listening to his counsel. Charles indignantly denied that he
was Digby's puppet, sharply rebuked Rupert, Willys and the
rest, and refused to alter his decision.

Rupert returned to Belvoir at the end of October, whence
he wrote to the Parliament at Westminster asking for a pass
to go abroad. The reply which he received was that a pass would
be granted only if he promised never to serve the King again.

That promise Rupert would not give. Leaving Belvoir, he fought his way back through Worcester to Woodstock, north of Oxford. As soon as Charles himself returned to Oxford, he ordered Legge's release but not his reinstatement. Eventually, under pressure from Legge and from his friends the Duke and Duchess of Richmond, Rupert wrote letters of apology to the

William Legge, close friend of Rupert.

King acknowledging his errors and in particular expressing deep regret for his behaviour at Newark. His first letter was thought not to be strong enough and he had to write another, which exemplifies his command of the English language: 'I am sorry', he wrote, 'to understand by Will Legge that yor Ma^{ti} hath not that satisfaction wch I endeavoured to give yor Ma^{ti} in my last letter, and conceived to have given you therein; and now I shall once again freely acknowledge my Errors; and humbly intreat yor Ma^{ti} to consider me by the better and more lastinge expressions of my Zeale and affection, and to pardon what is done amiss and to accept it when it cannot err wch is my humble duty and service to yor Ma^{ti} in wch way be pleased to command and dispose as you shall think fit.' Charles is said to have accepted this apology with tears in his eyes. So Rupert and Maurice were allowed to come back from Woodstock to Oxford at the end of 1645.

But Rupert was not restored to any official position, though he remained on friendly terms with the King. The royalist cause was now hopeless; after a victorious campaign in the south-west, which compelled the Prince of Wales to leave Cornwall for France, General Fairfax returned to blockade Oxford. In the spring of 1646 Charles resolved to make his way in disguise to the headquarters of the Scottish army in the hope that he could persuade its leaders to intervene on his behalf. Though Rupert offered to accompany Charles, he distrusted the Scots and was opposed to the whole idea. At his request the King recorded on paper that Rupert was against the undertaking. Charles left Oxford on 27 April; two months later the city surrendered to Fairfax.

In accordance with the terms of the treaty of surrender permission was given to Rupert and Maurice to go abroad at once or to stay peacefully wherever they liked for six months, provided it was not within twenty miles of London. Fairfax granted permission for them to go to Oatlands, a royal palace near London in Surrey, because they wanted to meet their eldest brother who was again in England. Parliament regarded this as a breach of faith; it therefore insisted that Rupert should leave the country with Maurice inside ten days; so he sailed from Dover to join Queen Henrietta Maria and the Prince of Wales in Paris.

Looking back upon Rupert's career as a commander on land, the first point to emerge is how his military career was affected by his character. Rupert was young and had all the impetuosity of youth. Though George Washington was a brigadier at the same age as Rupert when he retired, he had not yet distinguished himself in any battle. Napoleon had also only been appointed a brigadier at that age, though his rise was meteoric. Rupert's tactlessness and dislike of criticism were a handicap to him because he was not always able to exact the unquestioning loyalty of his subordinate officers. When he temporarily replaced Lord Byron as military commander at Chester with his friend, Will Legge, he was inviting trouble. His almost pathological distrust of Digby and Wilmot also damaged harmony; in fact both men were faithful to the King and had sensible military ideas. Indeed Wilmot, like Lord Astley, Lord Goring and other noble officers, had at least as much experience in war as Rupert had himself when he arrived in England; they could therefore reasonably resent Rupert's being put over them, attributing it to favouritism.

But Rupert had many good qualities. He was sober in his habits, no chaser after women, and dedicated to his profession. The only suggestion that he was a debauchee comparable with Goring or Wilmot came from his dallying in Bristol after the shock of his defeat at Marston Moor. His recklessness in battle has been unfairly exaggerated. Other famous generals such as Marshal Foch have taken for their motto 'toujours l'attaque'. Rupert's method of striking hard at the earliest opportunity, first practised by him when he was on his way to Lemgo, stood him in good stead. His cavalry charge at Powick Bridge in 1642 earned him a reputation that struck fear into the hearts of his enemies. Similarly at Edgehill in 1642, Bristol in 1643, and Newark in 1644, his willingness to lead his men into the attack at whatever danger to his own person contributed to substantial victories. In more recent times generals have preferred to direct battles from behind, like the Duke of Plaza-toro in *The Gondoliers* who 'found it more exciting'.

One of Rupert's difficulties was that no clearly defined chain of command existed. He was given ill-defined commissions and commands before he was appointed captain-general. Even then his right to take his own decisions or to obtain clear instructions from the King was by no means plain. It was a bit of nonsense that although he was in effect commander-in-chief, he was nominally under the orders of a fourteen-year-old boy. King Charles adopted the rather pusillanimous course of not giving Rupert 'peremptory commands' but merely strong suggestions about his 'pleasure'. The only time when the King did give him a 'peremptory command' was before the Battle of Marston Moor, and that proved to be absolutely disastrous. If the King had allowed Rupert his own way, he would have marched on London immediately after the Battle of Edgehill, he would have stormed Gloucester in 1643, he would not have fought the Battle of Naseby in 1645, and he would have brought the King with him into Bristol later in the same year. If his advice had been followed on these occasions Charles might conceivably have won the First Civil War. On the other hand, Sir Philip Warwick, who took the view in his memoirs that had it not been for the bad behaviour of others of the King's generals the 'excellent Prince Rupert' might have won the war, also admitted that Rupert had 'a little sharpness of temper' and 'uncommunicableness in society or council': in other words, his advice might have been more willingly received had the Prince been a man of tact.

However, a commander-in-chief always has the problem that if he is not the political head of the government which is fighting the war his strategic instincts are likely to be overruled on purely political grounds (as were Lord Alexander's during the Second World War). The reason why Alexander the Great, Julius Caesar, King Henry V of England, the first Duke of Marlborough and Napoleon I all won so many victories was that they were for the most part carrying out their own long-term aims. Marlborough was not, it is true, the head of the British government when he won his famous victories; but he was the military heir of King William III and for eight years a leading and highly influential member of Queen Anne's cabinets. Rupert was a foreigner fighting loyally for his uncle, but it was hard for him – indeed almost impossible – to understand the pretensions of the 'rebels' who claimed that they too were fighting for the King – and Parliament. Charles was at first anxious not to alienate his subjects by pressing them too severely. That was why he reproved Rupert for his attitude to the mayor of Leicester in 1642; that was why he would not allow Rupert to attack London earlier than he did in the same year; that was why he refused to storm Gloucester in 1643.

Another illuminating facet of the relations between Charles and Rupert is that whereas Rupert was the better strategist, Charles was arguably more successful in the field. The King deserves credit for the victories at Cropredy Bridge and Lostwithiel and for the relief of Hereford. Rupert, on the other hand, by failing to discipline his cavalry in the way that Oliver Cromwell did, threw away the chances of a complete victory at the Battles of Edgehill and Naseby. But he proved himself a versatile commander: his sieges of Cirencester, Lichfield and Bristol demonstrated his capacity to make the best use of his artillery and of mining. Had his advice been accepted, not only might Gloucester have been speedily stormed but the Earl of Essex might have been defeated. This was another example of the political fetters that were imposed upon his actions. The King adopted the rather illogical view that though he was engaged in a war against his own subjects, he must hurt them as little as possible in the process. The Battle of Marston Moor ought to have been fought differently – that is to say by Rupert attacking the opposing army when it was marching away to Tadcaster – or not at all. Still, Rupert's deployment of his troops on the field of battle was sound enough; the result might have gone the other way if Lord Byron had obeyed orders. It could be contended that Rupert's essential weakness was that he was not a successful disciplinarian, even if Warwick thought otherwise.

Rupert's fundamental difficulty then was that it was in a civil war that he had to display his talents as a soldier; for even though he was the King's nephew, the aristocratic adherents of the monarch were reluctant to take orders unquestioningly from a youthful German prince who knew little about English society. Men like Wilmot, Goring and Dyve did not scruple to evade or disobey his orders. Whatever he may have intended, Charles I failed to back him; he preferred to divide and rule. Lastly it did not help Rupert in his efforts to enforce his leadership that his elder brother was known to be on friendly terms with the opposing side.

How far were the parliamentarians justified when they

A

DIALOGUE

between the

DEVIL & Prince *RUPERT*,

Written at the

Leaguer before *Chester* upon
R u p e r t s coming to relieve
the said City.

Published, that those that now
are, or hereafter shall engage, as Caterers,
for the same master, might by this
general debenter be the better assured
to receive all their Arrears both
old and new.

Written by *E. B.*

June 23 ·   *1649*

London, Printed for *T. B.*

A broadsheet
portraying Rupert as
the perpetrator of
heinous crimes.

114

pictured Rupert as a brutal German? He was subjected to every kind of opprobrium: 'the most bloody and mischievous of all the Cavaliers', 'the Robber Prince', 'the flying dragon prince', 'the ungrateful viper'. He was asked: 'How many towns hast thou fired? How many virgins hast thou ruined? How many godly ministers hast thou killed? How many thousands hast thou plundered from his Majesty's best and most obedient subjects? How many innocents hast thou slain? How many oaths hast thou belched out against God and his people?' Early in 1643 Rupert published a declaration in his own defence against such calumnies, which he began by saying that it must be strange 'to see me in print, my known disposition being so contrary to this scribbling age'. Denying that he had been responsible for deliberately killing or inflicting cruelty upon women and children, he instanced the way in which the Roundheads ill treated ladies of quality. He admitted that accidents will happen, that his soldiers occasionally lost control over themselves. He argued that it was right to take money and arms away from rebels. Finally he repudiated the suggestion that he or his men were 'papist monsters'; had he not undergone perils both in the Netherlands and Germany on behalf of the Protestant cause?

The truth was that the soldiers on both sides were liable to get out of hand when assaulting towns, once a breach had been effected. Bristol in 1643 and Leicester in 1645 suffered from plundering and fortuitous killing of civilians. But Fairfax's men equally lost their control after the second siege of Bristol – indeed Fairfax apologized for the insolence of his men. In the same year, Cromwell stormed Burghley House, and many of those who resisted were put to the sword and the house given over to plunder. The most notorious atrocities on the Roundhead side occurred after Rupert had ceased to serve the Stuarts on land, following Cromwell's assaults on Drogheda and Wexford in Ireland – this was the second time his men had got completely out of hand – and after Monck's capture of Dundee in 1651 when civilians including women were killed, the governor murdered in cold blood, and plundering carried out in defiance of orders. It is perfectly true that according to the then recognized rules of war a garrison could be put to the sword if it continued fighting after a breach had been made in the walls.

But, as we have seen, Rupert did not insist on exercising this right either at Bristol in 1643 or at Leicester in 1645. Finally, it has to be accepted that throughout modern history rebels have invariably been punished with ruthlessness. No evidence exists to show that Rupert was more brutal or vindictive than other generals in the Civil Wars—including the parliamentarian commander-in-chief who had two brave royalist officers executed in cold blood after the siege of Colchester in 1648.

Such were Rupert's qualities and defects as a military commander. Like Cromwell, who is also accepted as a great general, Rupert had to plan and fight his battles in a comparatively restricted area and was bound by political and economic considerations. Cromwell of course was never defeated, though he was once or twice repulsed. If Rupert had enjoyed a free hand in the determination of strategy, he might well have won the war for his uncle.

Chapter Seven

⚜

THE ADMIRAL

On 19 July 1646 Rupert joined the Prince of Wales and his mother at St Germain. Prince Charles was only sixteen, but his searing experiences during the First Civil War had already made a man of him. Rupert had always had friendly relations with him and was much respected by his young cousin; Henrietta Maria, as has been observed, held changeable views about Rupert. In 1643 she had been jealous of his authority over her husband, and had also distrusted his military judgement. But her political influence has been exaggerated. King Charles would hardly have suggested that Rupert accompany her to the south-west of England in 1644 unless their relations had been amicable. Although the King dismissed Rupert from his military offices at the end of 1645, Charles was subsequently to write to his wife when he became a prisoner of the parliamentarians – as he did in August 1646 – recommending his nephew to her and assuring her that he was entirely loyal and courageous even if his 'passions may sometimes make him mistakes'.

Rupert was scarcely the man to sit on his heels, so while he awaited any further realistic opportunity to serve the royalist cause he enlisted in the French army, was appointed *maréchal de camp* (equivalent to a brigadier), and given command of the English in French pay.

The interminable war between France and Spain, which had begun in 1635 and was not to end until 1659, was largely fought in the southern Netherlands. At this stage the Spaniards were getting the best of it, but Rupert managed to take the town of La Bassée. During the campaign Robert Holmes, an Irish gentleman who was about the same age as Rupert and was to become one of his closest friends, was wounded in the leg, while Rupert, who was caught in an ambush, received a head wound. When Marshal Gassion, the commander under whom Rupert fought, said to him, '*Je suis bien fasché que vous êtes blessé*', the Prince replied '*Et moi aussi*'. He had a letter from his uncle, now a prisoner of the New Model Army at Hampton Court, saying that he had been glad to hear that he was recovered from his wound and 'assuring him that, next to my children (I say next) I shall have the most care of you and shall take the first opportunity to employ you or have your company'.

A chance to help the royalist cause presented itself to Rupert in 1648. The royal navy (much of it built by Charles I out of the proceeds of ship money) had gone over to the side of Parliament at the outbreak of the First Civil War. The Earl of Warwick had then been appointed admiral of the fleet by Parliament, but in 1645 he resigned for political reasons, being succeeded by a regular naval officer, William Batten. At the beginning of 1648 it was planned to replace Batten, who was a strong Presbyterian and disliked the seizure of the King by the army, which he thought might lead to the monarch's execution, by Colonel Thomas Rainsborough, a political extremist with republican and democratic views and a man of 'insufferable pride'. Apparently partly because of their distrust of Rainsborough and partly for political reasons, the crews of ten warships stationed in the Downs mutinied in May 1648, after a second civil war had broken out on land, and decided to go over to the royalists. As soon as the Prince of Wales and Prince Rupert heard the news of the revolt they travelled by way of Calais from Paris to Helvoetsluys at the mouth of the Meuse where the mutinous ships had arrived. Batten himself reached there later in the *Constant Warwick*, an armed merchantman with thirty guns of which he was the part owner, whereupon Prince Charles promptly knighted him.

The question then arose as to what was the best use to be made of the revolted fleet. Rupert was in favour of sailing to the Isle of Wight where the King was now a prisoner (having escaped from Hampton Court). That was surely the most sensible course, but not the most practicable, because the seamen sought an operation which would yield prizes. When they sailed for England in July, with the young Prince of Wales in com-

Robert Rich, Earl of Warwick, admiral of the parliamentarian navy.

mand, Lord Willoughby of Parham as vice-admiral, and Batten as rear-admiral, no specific strategic plan had been adopted, although it was quite a formidable fleet, amounting to to eighteen vessels (including a few captured and converted merchant ships) with 312 guns. Merchant ships coming out of the Thames were taken as prizes, and an unsuccessful effort was made to prevent the recapture of Deal and Walmer Castles in Kent, which had temporarily been held by the royalists.

Meanwhile Parliament, alarmed at the mutiny (although the

war had been going well for them on land), had hastily recalled
the Earl of Warwick to the command. Warwick, with part of
the navy carrying 318 guns – the rest of it was stationed at
Portsmouth – was challenged to battle by the Prince of Wales
near the mouth of the Thames. Warwick declined action, a
strong wind blew up, and the Prince found himself short of
supplies and ammunition, so he led his fleet back to Holland.
As it returned another fleet was spotted, which Rupert, who
was on board the admiral's ship with Prince Charles, thought
must be the Portsmouth ships sailing to join up with Warwick's
main force. As was his way, Rupert favoured immediate action;
but unfortunately for him the other vessels turned out to be
merely coalships.

On reaching Holland Charles and .Rupert went to The
Hague, presumably in search of moral and material support.
Warwick, with the bulk of his fleet (including the ships from
Portsmouth), followed the royalist vessels across the North Sea.
Batten and his friend Captain Jordan now threw up the sponge
and sailed away in the armed merchantman which they jointly
owned, having accepted an amnesty from the Earl of Warwick.
Prince Charles then invited Rupert to take charge of the fleet.
Rupert modestly said that he would accept the command under
Charles's younger brother James, who bore the title of lord high
admiral. But Charles insisted that Rupert should have the
fullest powers with the right to raise the royal standard on his
flagship.

The immediate problem was to get the ships safely into the
river Meuse, which was linked by a sluice with the outer
harbour in the North Sea, so that they should not suffer damage
in the autumn storms and could be refitted for operations in
the following year. For a time there was a contest between
Rupert and Warwick as to who should haul his ships through
the sluice. In the end most of the royalist ships managed to get
through, while Warwick's fleet remained anchored only a short
distance away in the outer harbour. But the Dutch naturally
had no intention of allowing a battle to start in their home
waters. The Dutch admiral, Maarten van Tromp, arrived with
a strong squadron, anchored between the contending fleets, and
prohibited all acts of hostility. So the only trouble that arose
was in squabbles between the rival sets of sailors in the neigh-

bouring Dutch taverns. By 21 November Warwick decided he dared stay no longer, so he took his fleet back to England. Rupert was thus able to concentrate on refitting and raising recruits for a new campaign.

In the Middle Ages battles at sea had consisted of ships grappling each other so that the crews could board and enter enemy vessels and capture them by hand-to-hand fighting. In Tudor times battles were fought with guns: the Spanish armada was defeated because the English vessels were more agile and the guns of longer range. Being a pacific monarch, King James I had demobilized most of the navy and refused to grant letters of marque enabling owners of armed merchant vessels to act as privateers – that is, as licensed pirates. Charles I inherited some twenty-five warships, but the fleets that unsuccessfully attacked the Spaniards and the French at the outset of his reign consisted largely of hired and armed merchant ships. Admiral Sir John Penington, who was one of Charles's better admirals, held the opinion that properly equipped men-of-war could make mincemeat out of armed merchantmen because the guns of the latter, being insufficiently stabilized, were virtually useless. The King therefore set about building more warships. It was for this reason that he levied ship money, a tax which was so unpopular that it ·is generally considered to be one of the immediate causes of the Civil War.

Charles's ship money fleet amounted to thirty-five vessels when the Civil War began. The enormous naval expansion which took place during the following twenty years is demonstrated by the fact that when Charles II returned to England in 1660 he inherited a navy of over two hundred warships. By then the separation between men-of-war and trading ships was complete. The average warship was a short squat vessel of a few hundred tons with a forecastle mounted in the stern, which was the highest part of the ship, and a bow which was the lowest part and had to be protected from the lashing of the waves. In contemporary illustrations the bowsprit jutting up easily distinguishes the front of a warship from the elaborately decorated stern. Generally these ships were two-deckers with an upper or poop deck the width of which was about two-thirds of the depth of the water-line. Guns would be mounted in the forecastle, while other cannon lined both sides of the ship, the heaviest on the lower deck. Guns would also be placed at each end of the ship, with a total of some thirty to ninety guns on the larger warships. (Ships of the line were those which carried twenty-five guns or more, and were classified as first to fourth rates.) The rapidity of fire of these guns was only about ten to twelve cannonades an hour, but when a broadside could be let off by simultaneously firing all the guns on one side of the ship it amounted to a formidable salvo. Their range did not exceed 400 yards. Even at that range accurate fire was difficult because it was impossible to obtain a steady gun platform, and because of the difficulty of penetrating the thick oak of which warships were constructed.

The pride of Charles I's navy was the *Sovereign of the Seas*, completed in 1637, which had three decks, over a hundred guns and weighed some 1,500 tons. But, like the battleships of Admiral Jellicoe's days, such a relative monster was more impressive than practicable. Indeed Charles was criticized for not building smaller and lighter ships – frigates or fifth and sixth rates – which were easier to handle; for the naval armament of ships was heavy in relation to tonnage and caused the ships to roll. The stowage of guns often caused leaks. Despite Admiral Penington's view, frigates could be fashioned out of suitable merchantmen captured as prizes; for it was found much easier to strengthen them and add forecastles to carry more guns than to raise the money required to build new men-of-war. Most ships had three masts and stood high out of the sea. Their sails could be increased by top-sails; their speed averaged ten knots. But some of them, such as the *Constant Reformation*, which was to be Rupert's flagship, were unable to work their guns on the lower deck in a rough or even a moderate sea.

Able-bodied seamen were paid at the relatively high rate of 22s 6d a week; they were given rations of meat, biscuit, cheese and beer, and inevitably suffered from scurvy. They did not receive their pay until the end of the voyage, and not always then, but they depended much more on hopes of sharing in the value of captured vessels and blood money. Because of the irregular pay and harsh discipline of the navy, service on board privateers and in the ordinary mercantile marine – for instance on the ships of the East India Company – was more popular and profitable. But naval officers were quite generously paid, and they received a higher proportion of prize money than the men in accordance with their rank.

The normal tactics of naval warfare consisted in gaining the weather gauge – that is to say ensuring that the wind was blowing from astern so that the sailing ships could run before it in the direction in which their captains wished to go while the enemy, if they were to attack, would have to beat into the wind. Once the weather gauge had been gained the ships would be spaced out and each would deliver their broadsides on the enemy ship to which it was immediately opposed; then, if necessary, they would continue the attack by sending the leading units of the fleet to the rear and filing past the enemy again. That was excellent in theory, but in practice most naval battles were *mêlées* or dog fights. Dashing and individual manoeuvre was more attractive to a man like Rupert in his salad days. Indeed it was laid down by the Earl of Lindsey, who was one of Charles I's admirals, that no ships should presume to assault the enemy admiral's, vice-admiral's or rear-admiral's vessels 'but only myself, my vice-admiral and my rear-admiral', while other ships were to match themselves against their equals and not waste their powder on smaller vessels. But in fact the inaccuracy of the naval guns – which required thirteen movements for loading, were often ranged too low on the waterline, and even on warships were rarely stable – meant that direct hits were seldom fatal; and the limited range of cannon was also an obstacle to complete success. The sinking of, say, five sizeable ships in a battle was therefore exceptional. In time it was discovered that fireships – small expendable vessels which could be towed downwind, ignited and allowed to drift on to their victims – were more destructive than broadsides, while smaller guns loaded with chain shot were more harassing to the enemy. The effective employment of fireships of course required the capture of the weather gauge. For a naval victory that was almost essential. 'First I will strive to get the wind if I be to leeward,' wrote the Earl of Lindsey, 'and so shall the whole fleet in due order do the like.'

The appointment of Rupert as admiral was not as surprising as it might seem. The principal requirement of a naval commander was a knowledge of artillery, since the guns used on the fleet – culverins (18-pounders), demi-culverins and demi-

General George Monck, who fought for the royalists in the first civil war, but after the execution of Charles I served the Commonwealth both as a military and naval commander. He was to play a large part in the restoration of Charles II to the English throne and was to be the colleague of Rupert in the second Anglo-Dutch war.

cannon (9-pounders) and sakers (5-pounders) – were the same as those employed for land warfare. Both Colonel Robert Blake and Colonel George Monck, who were made admirals or 'generals-at-sea' by Parliament, were artillerymen of ripe experience.

Rupert had a tricky time before Warwick's final withdrawal. In the middle of September 1648 he had 'caused the ships to be unrigged and in expectation of the frost which must certainly force the Parliament fleet to quit the road'. But Warwick stayed longer than Rupert had expected, while the Dutch squadron had withdrawn at the beginning of November. As a precaution Rupert removed the guns from his ships to protect the harbour. Meanwhile Warwick succeeded in regaining three of the ships that had mutinied, the *Satisfaction*, which had twenty guns, and two smaller vessels. The crew of the *Antelope* was also restless. This was an antiquated ship, which had been built in 1619 but carried thirty-eight guns. Rupert acted boldly when his orders were disobeyed, went aboard the ship, caught hold of one of the ringleaders 'and held him overboard, as if he would throw him into the sea'. That stopped the rot. Later fresh food was withheld from the *Antelope*, its guns were sold or transferred to other vessels, the mutineers on board were removed, and the ship's contents disposed of for what they would fetch.

Despite the coming of winter, after Warwick's departure Rupert sent out raiding frigates to capture English merchant vessels as prizes out of which to pay and provide for his fleet. On 18 January 1649 Walter Strickland, Parliament's ambassador extraordinary at The Hague, wrote to the Speaker of the House of Commons saying, 'I am sorry what I must tell to you that the revolted ships come in daily with great prizes . . . It is no great joy to me to see our merchants beggared.'

Rupert was left with eight ships under his command: the *Constant Reformation* (45 guns), the *Convertine* (40), the *Charles* (40), the *Swallow* (36), the *Roebuck* (30), the *James* (28), the *Thomas* (24) and the *Blackmoor Lady* (18). As admiral Rupert flew his flag on the *Constant Reformation*; his brother Maurice as vice-admiral was aboard the *Convertine*; while Sir John Mennes, a naval officer of much experience, was appointed rear-admiral and commanded the *Swallow*. The three flagships lacked sufficient crews: in December 1648 the total number of seamen available to Rupert was eight hundred. But with the aid of Lord Hopton, intensive recruiting, refitting and provisioning was carried out. The Prince of Wales also gave what help he could. Hopton told Rupert at the beginning of 1649 that he hoped to have everything ready by the spring. But Rupert did much better than that. Three weeks later the Prince of Wales was informed that the ships were ready at Helvoetsluys. He wrote from The Hague to congratulate his cousin and to say that he would never forget his great care and industry, while Sir Edward Hyde (who as Earl of Clarendon was rather hard on

King Charles's
execution: a woodcut
from a contemporary
broadsheet.

Rupert in his classic *History of the Rebellion*) reported that the
preservation of the fleet must be entirely ascribed to him. In
a letter written at the time, he said that the Prince 'hath
expressed greater temper and discretion in it than you can
imagine', adding that after Batten and Jordan 'played the
rogues with us' Rupert had taken charge and 'with unwearied
pains and toil put all things in reasonable order'.

Apart from this small fleet the only hope which the royalists
clung to in January 1649, when King Charles I was being tried
for his life by the remnants of the Westminster Parliament, was
Ireland. The Marquis of Ormonde, a loyal servant of the King,
who in 1647 had resigned his lord lieutenancy of Ireland and
handed over the problem of securing the country to the London
authorities, had returned there in October 1648 as the King's
lord lieutenant with instructions to negotiate an agreement
between the royalists and the native Irish. Ormonde landed

in Cork without difficulty and soon set up his headquarters in Dublin. As the King was no longer at liberty, Queen Henrietta Maria and the Prince of Wales took it upon themselves to order Rupert to lead his squadron to southern Ireland so as to lend his support to Ormonde.

Rupert set sail for Ireland on 21 January 1649 with a favourable wind. His ships of the line, four frigates and one prize were accompanied by three Dutch merchant ships, which gave the impression that his squadron was larger than it really was. That was how he successfully bluffed his way past Dover. His faithful brother Maurice was given charge of three of the ships, which after capturing prizes rendezvoused safely with Rupert's ships at Kinsale.

It was not until the end of February that Rupert learned that Charles I had been executed and that the Prince of Wales had succeeded his father as King. In his new capacity Charles II at once confirmed Rupert in his position as admiral and also conferred that honorific appointment of master of the horse, the office which had been taken away from him after the surrender of Bristol. Rupert was determined to avenge what he called 'the bloody and inhuman murder' of Charles I by doing his best to restore the late king's son to the English throne. He confessed that he would have preferred not to be employed as admiral since slanders were circulated about his motives for accepting the post such as that he had taken it on for the profits that might be made out of it. He would gladly have occupied a more modest position had not the young king insisted upon his taking the naval command.

So far as Ireland was concerned it was obvious that Rupert was in a delicate position. As a prince he could scarcely be made subordinate to Ormonde; on the other hand, Ormonde, whose knowledge of Ireland was hereditary and comprehensive, could not be asked to obey Rupert, who knew nothing whatever about the country. Ormonde's biographer observed that Rupert 'had a parcel of worthless creatures about him, who endeavoured to sow jealousies between him and the Lord Lieutenant', and complained that the fleet gave Ormonde no help. It is of course true that Rupert was – or had in the past shown himself to be – proud and touchy. But it is doubtful if Rupert was jealous or failed to do what he could to assist Ormonde. Ormonde himself

wrote to Charles II (in February 1649): 'If any there be that make it their design to beget misunderstandings in me to his Highness they will quickly find their art misapplied.'

Soon after his arrival at Kinsale Rupert dispatched five ships to the relief of the Scilly Isles, which had been a centre of royalist privateering but were now threatened by the parliamentarians. Supplies were landed and a party of soldiers left in command.

Kinsale in the
seventeenth century.

Rupert also sent out frigates to prey on English merchant ships
so that he was able to augment his fleet and lay up stocks in
the port of Kinsale and neighbouring harbours. The government of the English republic or Free Commonwealth, which
gradually came into being after Charles I's death, was soon
stung into action. Three generals-at-sea were appointed in
February. Colonel Edward Popham, a Somersetman, had

129

active experience of naval warfare; the other two, Blake and Richard Deane, had served with distinction as colonels but had less knowledge of the sea than Popham. Blake came of a mercantile family in Somerset, Deane was essentially an artilleryman but had made sea voyages in his youth. In April Popham set sail and carried out a reconnaissance to the west of the Channel. On a misty day he ran into the *Charles*, one of the ships dispatched by Rupert to the Scillies. After an hour's fight the captain of the *Charles* surrendered. The other ships got safely back to Kinsale. Rupert then realized that he was in for a difficult time, but optimistically claimed that if the worst came to the worst he would take the whole fleet to the Scillies, which, he said, 'I doubt not ere long to see...a second Venice'.

By the middle of June the republican generals-at-sea had begun a blockade of Kinsale, but they were unable to keep their ships, which outnumbered Rupert's, constantly at sea because of bad weather. This they blamed upon providence, though they were grateful also that providence kept the royalist ships in port and thus prevented them from capturing more mercantile shipping. Rupert himself visited Waterford and other nearby towns during June to recruit soldiers and sailors for his fleet. He also dispatched weapons and what money he could spare from the sale of prizes for the use of Ormonde's army. However, he had too few ships to do what the Marquis would have liked, which was to protect the harbour at Dublin from an enemy assault by sea.

By the late summer the whole situation in Ireland had changed. Ormonde was defeated on 2 August at the Battle of Rathmines and was forced to evacuate Dublin. A fortnight later Oliver Cromwell, who was both commander-in-chief of an efficient expeditionary force and the Commonwealth's nominee as lord lieutenant of the country, landed near Dublin. In September he captured Drogheda, north of Dublin; then, turning south, he conquered Wexford. Terrified by these two ferocious sieges, the garrison of Cork, ten miles east of Kinsale, hastened to change sides. Long before this Rupert had written to Ormonde warning him that he would have to sail away from Kinsale in September – in any case there was little point in his remaining there – for he might be attacked by land as well as by sea. By the autumn he reckoned that the weather would have

JOYFULL
NEVVES
For the Citizens of
LONDON

From the Princes Fleet at Sea ; Wherein is communicated, the The full particulars of a great Victory obtained , the difpierfing of the Navy, and beating them into feverall Harbours ; the taking of thirty fhips and Frigats, two hundred pieces of Ordnance, and above four hundred prifoners. The rifing of a new Army in *Ireland*, for Prince *Charles* confifting of twenty thoufand and their Declaration and Letter fent to his Highnefs fhewing their prefent Refolution and Intentions. With the further proceedings of the Prince, and the Scots, the preparations againft England, and the buying of ten thoufand Armes in Holland.

Printed in the year Year, 1649.

The events related in this enthusiastic broadsheet seem to be largely fabrication.

deteriorated and a favourable breeze might enable him to escape the parliamentarian blockade. That was in fact what happened, though not until mid-October. Blake, who was now in command of the blockaders, was driven back by a storm to refit in Milford Haven.

On 20 October Rupert departed from Kinsale. His ships had been careened during the summer, but the whole operation had been disappointing. According to a diarist who accompanied Rupert on his naval voyages (probably one of his naval captains, for he was obviously a master of nautical terminology), Rupert himself would have been prepared to risk a battle. But his council of war, consisting in part of professional officers, was firmly against it, the Irish were unfriendly, and supplies of food and wages for the seamen began to run out. So reluctantly Rupert disbanded the recruits which he had collected with so much energy. With seven ships, the *Constant Reformation*, the *Swallow* and the *Convertine* plus four frigates, he made for Spain across the choppy Bay of Biscay, capturing one or two prizes on the way. The Spanish authorities, who were to be the first to recognize the republican regime in England, were not enthusiastic over Rupert's arrival. He took on supplies and sailed away to Portugal. The King of Portugal, the young John IV, who was fighting Spain to secure the independence of his kingdom, welcomed Rupert to Lisbon, allowing him to bring his ships into the calm and safety of the river Tagus.

While he was off Ireland, Rupert had lost several ships, including a captured frigate aboard which was his old friend Will Legge, who had been taken prisoner. He had also, as has been noted, lost the *Charles* to Popham. On the other hand, he had captured a vessel which was suitable for conversion into a 36-gun warship – he named it the *Second Charles* – and when he reached the Tagus he added the *Black Prince*, a prize which carried thirty guns, to his squadron. Thus in net terms his naval losses were small or negligible. But a cumulative lack of supplies and money compelled him to reduce his commitments, so he disarmed the *Convertine*, which was an old ship built in 1616, and sold it and the *Blackmoor Lady* to help pay his way. By the time he sailed away from Portugal in October 1649 he had only six ships left. With these he was to engage in his greatest exploit at sea, sailing halfway across the world.

✤

Chapter Eight

SAILING ACROSS
THE WORLD

A pleasing reception awaited Rupert in Portugal. John of Braganza, who had become king himself only after a national revolt against Spain in 1640, which was still continuing, did not as a *nouveau monarque* approve of a government executing an anointed sovereign and replacing him by a republic. During his stay in Kinsale Rupert had written to King John IV to see if he and his small fleet would be welcome there and had eventually obtained an encouraging reply. On their way to the Tagus Rupert and Maurice took three ships as prizes, two of which put up a good fight before capitulating. They withstood broadsides from the frigates, but when the ships of the line came up they surrendered.

The mouth of the Tagus was guarded by forts. A message from the King having invited Rupert's ships into the river, the guns from the forts let off a cheering salute. The squadron then anchored in Oeiras Bay. Rupert set out to be affable to the Portuguese. According to the diarist of his voyages, he 'began to show himself frequently amongst them, hunting daily, as though he suspected no danger, but making them his security: this, with his liberality and complaisance to all sorts of people, they having been accustomed to a Spanish gravity, were surprised by such unusual favours from so great a person...'

However, danger was looming up. The Commonwealth Council of State was by no means pleased with their generals-at-sea allowing Rupert to escape from Ireland. On 1 March Robert Blake left the Isle of Wight with a fleet carrying over 450 guns; he was accompanied by Charles Vane, the younger brother of Sir Henry Vane, who was treasurer of the navy. Charles Vane had been appointed a special envoy whose duty

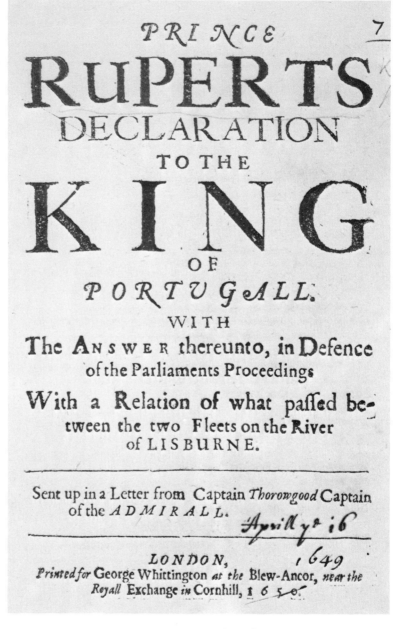

PRINCE 7

RUPERTS

DECLARATION

TO THE

KING

OF

PORTUGALL.

WITH

The Answer thereunto, in Defence
of the Parliaments Proceedings

With a Relation of what passed between the two Fleets on the River
of LISBURNE.

Sent up in a Letter from Captain *Thorowgood* Captain
of the *ADMIRALL.*

Aprill ye 16

LONDON, *1649*

Printed for George Whittington *at the* Blew-Ancor, *near the*
Royall Exchange *in* Cornhill, 1 6 5 0.

Rupert was initially welcomed by the Portuguese
king and populace . . .

... until the arrival of the English fleet under
Robert Blake put pressure on Portugal to surrender
him.

it was to obtain the recognition of the Commonwealth by Portugal and then to ask permission to exterminate what he
deemed a nest of pirates. But Blake did not await the result
of the diplomatic negotiations; he left Cascaes Bay, which he
had reached on 10 March, and tried to force his way into the
Tagus. The Portuguese forts fired their guns at his fleet, then
calm weather obliged him to anchor. King John said that the
guns had been fired without his orders. He also gave permission

135

for the republican fleet to enter the river if the weather appeared tempestuous. Blake promptly took advantage of this permission to enter Oeiras Bay, where he anchored two miles down the river from Rupert's squadron.

Vane now exerted increasing pressure on the Portuguese king, while Rupert sought an agreement that if he left the Tagus and put out to sea Blake would undertake not to follow him for three days. That was not acceptable. Soon Rupert found other friends. France had not yet recognized the Common-wealth, so when two French men-of-war entered the river they joined Rupert in spite of an attempt by Blake to prevent them. The situation that had occurred in the Meuse now repeated itself in the Tagus. The two fleets glared at one another while their crews mingled on the shore. A skirmish took place when, according to Rupert, Blake's men tried to kidnap him while he was hunting. Whether this was true or not, Rupert certainly believed that it was, and by way of revenge made an effort to blow up the *Leopard*, a vessel of fifty-six guns commanded by Blake's vice-admiral. Rupert ordered one of his sailors disguised as a Portuguese to smuggle on board a time-bomb concealed in a barrel of oil, but this piece of ingenuity was frustrated.

On 15 May Edward Popham left Plymouth with ships carry-ing 174 guns to reinforce Blake. Before he arrived Blake had impounded nine of the ships sailing in a Portuguese convoy setting out for Brazil. The excuse for his doing so was that they were owned by English merchants resident in Lisbon and manned by English seamen. That was the first of several attempts to replace the diplomatic glove by the iron fist. When Popham joined Blake they together outnumbered Rupert by about two to one. It was agreed that a demand should be sent to the Portuguese king to surrender Rupert's ships to them, warning King John that if he refused they would use force. But the King would not at that time be intimidated by gunboat diplomacy. The English generals-at-sea proceeded to lay hold of a number of Portuguese fishing boats. By way of retort the King prevented Blake buying either food or water for his men; so Blake had to detach his vice-admiral to collect supplies from Cadiz. In his absence Rupert, supported by the Portuguese navy, attempted to come out of the river. His idea was that the Portuguese warships should shield him from Blake's guns while he escaped. But Blake got the weather gauge and when the wind changed both sides tacked. Rupert was out-manoeuvred and compelled to return to his original anchorage.

In August the Council of State at Whitehall informed its admirals that it no longer wanted to tie up such a large part of the navy watching Rupert. That was sensible enough, for much privateering and piracy were taking place in home waters where French marauders were particularly active in seizing mercantile shipping. Popham then sailed back to England, leaving Blake to cope with Rupert. Four days later (on 11 September) Rupert again tried to get out to sea. But although it was foggy, Blake managed to locate Rupert's flagship and give him a broadside which shot down his fore-top-mast. Again Rupert was obliged to return to his anchorage in the river.

A week later the Portuguese fleet returned from Brazil. Blake decided to teach the Portuguese a lesson. In a battle which lasted three hours the Portuguese admiral had his main-mast shot away and had to retire, while the rear-admiral surrendered. Blake captured six other ships loaded with sugar. He then withdrew to Cadiz in order to refuel. Taking advantage of his absence, Rupert was at last able to escape. He could not in any case have stayed much longer, for the Portuguese would not have been able to withstand the pressure of the powerful English Commonwealth. The King's leading minister had long been urging him to give way to Blake. Rupert left Lisbon on 12 October 1650 with only six ships. The fleet made for the Straits of Gibraltar and the Mediterranean where there was hope of rich prizes. As soon as he learned the news, Blake, who had returned to Portugal with his frigates, went back to Cadiz to collect his flagships and gave chase.

When Rupert's fleet was forced out of the Tagus it had nowhere to go and no clear objectives to pursue. 'Misfortunes,' recorded the diarist, 'being no novelty to us, we plough the sea for a subsistence, and, being destitute of a port, we take the confines of the Mediterranean Sea for our harbour; poverty and despair being our companions, and revenge our guide.' Rupert's immediate purpose was to capture what ships he could belonging to the allies of his enemies, and if he spotted English ships which he could not seize, to destroy them so as to inflict damage upon the Commonwealth. Rupert successfully negotiated the Straits and sailed east along the southern coast of Spain.

Two prizes were taken immediately and added to the fleet while at Estepona, twenty miles east of Gibraltar, an English warship – captained by a Londoner named Morley whom Rupert suspected of complicity in the murder of Charles I – was disabled. One of Rupert's ships, the *Second Charles*, was now missing. He hoped to find it at Tetuan opposite Spain in North Africa, but as it was not there the squadron returned to the coast of Spain, reaching Malaga on 26 October. At Velez-Malaga, farther east, Rupert arrogantly demanded of the Spanish governor that he should surrender the English ships anchored there as rebels. The governor refused; an attempt by Rupert to send in a fireship was frustrated, so he moved on to Montril whence he sent a light vessel (known as a caravel) which succeeded in setting three English ships on fire.

But now Nemesis, in the shape of Admiral Blake, was on the way. A storm separated the flagships commanded by Rupert and Maurice from the four other vessels, which tried to take shelter in Cartagena. The crew of one of them mutinied and it was captured by Blake; another ran ashore three leagues east of Cartagena, was set on fire, and blown up. The other two ships were forced on to the shore at Cartagena Bay by a sudden squall which staved in their bilges thus damaging them fatally. Blake required the Spaniards to hand over what remained of them – their guns, anchors and furniture – to him.

Meanwhile Rupert and Maurice had reached Formentara in the Balearic Islands, where, ignorant of the loss of all their other ships, they left a message ordering their captains to rendezvous off Sardinia. Then another storm separated the two brothers from each other. Maurice succeeded in capturing a valuable prize, which he brought into Toulon on 25 November. France was then in the throes of a civil war (known as the Second Fronde or Fronde of the Princes); and Toulon at that time sided with the Prince of Condé against the government, directed by Cardinal Mazarin. Possibly out of friendly feelings towards a fellow royal prince in rebellion against the English republic, Maurice was welcomed. The magistrates and the French naval officers there vied with each other in showing courtesy. But Maurice was so worried about the fate of Rupert

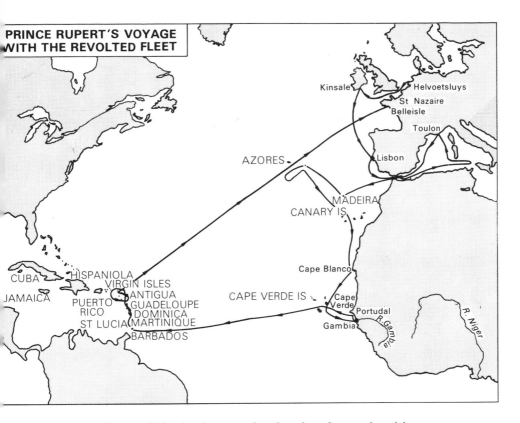

PRINCE RUPERT'S VOYAGE WITH THE REVOLTED FLEET

that he declined all invitations and refused to leave the ship. However, towards the end of December Rupert eventually arrived safely at Toulon. 'I need not express', wrote the diarist, 'the joy of their embraces after so long and tedious an absence, with the uncertainty of each other's safety ... who, after so long a time of hardship endured through the malice of enemies, the raging of the wind and seas, now found themselves locked in each other's arms in a place of safety.'

At Toulon Rupert and Maurice at last learned of the disaster at Cartagena, for one of the captains whose ship had been lost had been released from prison by the Spaniards on parole. Another of Rupert's naval captains also turned up at Toulon. Accusations and counter-accusations followed. Rupert rejected the idea of holding a court martial; but the captain whose misconduct he most suspected was dismissed from his service. Now a new squadron had somehow to be constructed.

Of the warships that left Portugal only the *Constant Reformation* and the *Swallow* were left. But Rupert managed to borrow some money to buy another ship, which was known as the *Honest Seaman*. He was also joined by a royalist naval captain named Craven who came to him from Marseilles in a ship called the *Speedwell*, touchingly rechristened the *Loyal Subject*. Finally Maurice's prize was converted into a warship and named the *Revenge*.

With these five ships Rupert turned west again, following the North African coast back to the Straits of Gibraltar. He escaped the attentions of a squadron under William Penn, which had been sent to find him, by spreading a story that he was sailing east towards the Levant. While they were in Toulon Rupert had received a letter from Queen Henrietta Maria in Paris offering him employment. But whether because he did not want to leave his brother or because he believed that Maurice was incapable of handling the ships without him, Rupert determined to stay with his improvised naval squadron. In the early summer of 1651 Rupert once more penetrated the Straits of Gibraltar, thus leaving the Mediterranean for the Atlantic. By this time he must already have covered more than a thousand miles of sea.

It was Rupert's ultimate intention to sail across the Atlantic to the West Indies where, according to his necessarily out-of-date information, Barbados and Antigua were still loyal to the royalists. Lord Willoughby of Parham, who had fought on the same side as Cromwell in Lincolnshire during 1643, and had then changed sides and been appointed vice-admiral of the royalist fleet in the course of the Second Civil War, was also the lessee proprietor of these islands; Charles II had dispatched him there in the spring of 1650 to be his representative. Though Willoughby succeeded for a time in asserting his position and strengthening the defences of the islands, Parliament at Westminster was determined to compel them to submit to its authority. An act was passed forbidding all trading with the royalist islands and later Admiral Sir George Ayscue was ordered to take a naval squadron to Barbados. So it happened that during 1651 a sort of race took place between Rupert and Ayscue to see who could get there first. But it was a leisurely race. Ayscue took a long time to fit out his squadron, while Rupert was

Sir George Ayscue, the parliamentarian admiral who raced Rupert to the West Indies.

obliged to search for adequate supplies of food and other stores before he could undertake the long and arduous voyage across the Atlantic.

In the spring of 1651, after sailing west along the coast of Andalusia, Rupert captured a Spanish ship bound from the Indies to Cadiz. This was legitimate enough in Rupert's eyes because the Spanish had recognized the Commonwealth the previous December and were therefore the allies of Charles II's enemies; moreover, he blamed them for the loss of four of his ships at Cartagena the year before and wanted revenge. He went first to Madeira to sell off his prize and buy supplies.

141

Madeira, being Portuguese, gave him a friendly reception, but was unable to meet all his needs. He therefore moved south to the Canary Islands, after leaving Madeira on 1 July, in the hope of capturing some English merchant ships there; but as none were to be found he sailed on to the Azores, also Portuguese, where he arrived about three weeks later. Before leaving Madeira the naval officers had learned with misgivings of Rupert's intention to sail to the West Indies; at a council of war they insisted that they must first go to the Azores, which were known then as the Western Isles, in order to fit out their ships, buy more food and, if possible, capture prizes.

In fact all this was accomplished. The governor of St Michael was extremely friendly and insisted on showing Rupert round the island. To smooth his path Rupert presented the governor with some guns and goods from the prizes which he had taken; in return he was allowed to send a party ashore to negotiate for supplies of food. After leaving St Michael Rupert captured another Spanish ship and brought it to the island of Terceira to the west. Although the governor of Terceira was less obliging than the governor of St Michael, Rupert was permitted to order wine and meat there.

After the departure from Terceira a sudden storm blew up which caused Rupert's flagship *Constant Reformation* to spring a leak. The crew was unable to pump out the water with a chain pump or to bale it out, or even to locate the leak. When they at last did so, an attempt was made to staunch the hole with one hundred and twenty pieces of raw beef, but the force of the sea dislodged the stanchion. Finally the guns were thrown overboard to lighten the warship, but early in the morning of 30 September it was known to be sinking. Desperately the sailors went on pumping out the water, determined to live or die with their ship. Prince Rupert resolved to go down with his men.

When Prince Maurice, who was aboard the *Swallow*, managed to get near, Rupert tried to give him his last instructions, but the roar of the wind and waves was such that they could not hear one another. Both the *Constant Reformation* and the *Swallow* had lost their pinnaces (light two-masted vessels that normally followed in the wake of warships and were used as scouts and tenders, but which had to be hoisted on board in such a rough sea if they were not to be wrecked). At four o'clock in the morning the lower chain pump on the *Constant Reformation* broke. The whole crew took the sacrament ready to die together. In the end, however, the *Honest Seaman* was able to dispatch a small light boat – a yawl – with a crew of five sailors to row it. They got hold of the end of a hawser but were compelled to let it go. Then they rowed close to a ladder lowered from the poop deck on the port side. Seeing the opportunity, the seamen on board the sinking ship begged Rupert to save himself. When he refused, they forced him into the boat, which was rowed safely back to the *Honest Seaman*. As soon as he reached the *Honest Seaman* Rupert ordered the yawl to return to carry out further rescues. But only a few men, including Rupert's flag captain, Fearnes, and Rupert's personal servants, were saved. Three hundred and thirty men perished while the whole of the precious cargo, so painfully collected, was lost.

Rupert was heart-broken. He transferred from the *Honest Seaman* to his brother's ship, the *Swallow*, and ordered him to take command of the two surviving ships (the *Revenge* and the *Loyal Subject* had been unable to keep company with the others). The diarist of the voyage wrote that Rupert concealed himself for a time on board his brother's ship because he was afraid that if the governors in the Western Isles learned of the loss of his flagship they might 'upon knowledge of so great a disaster' have changed their minds about allowing him to collect the supplies which he had ordered there.

When Rupert and Maurice limped back to the Azores more bad news awaited them at the island of Fayal, to the west of the group. For the *Loyal Subject*, which had been anchored there, had been driven away by a storm and holed to pieces on the rocks. (Captain Craven was to turn up in France years afterwards to apologize for this misfortune.) Furthermore the Portuguese governor of Fayal, who was something of a pirate himself, was afraid that the English would muscle in on his own preserves; he therefore imprisoned the officers Maurice had sent to purchase supplies on the island and refused to allow food or water to be loaded on board. Nor would the governor take any notice of Maurice's protests. Rupert was compelled to emerge from his hiding place. He took a strong line with the governor, warning him that he would inform his friend, the King of Portugal, about the affronts they had received. The governor crumpled, released his prisoners and allowed the supplies to be taken on board the three ships. So Rupert recovered his spirits. He and his ships sailed back to Terceira to collect more supplies and then on to St Michael for the same purpose; there at last he managed to induce his officers to agree to crossing the Atlantic to the West Indies. But he still needed to careen and sheathe his remaining vessels after their buffeting in the storms and to repair the rigging, buy further supplies of meat and, if possible, secure prizes. The year 1651 was nearly at its end when, sailing by way of the Canaries (where owing to the weather no prey could be found), Rupert reached the north-west coast of Africa.

Although the west of Africa was believed in Europe to be a land of milk and honey – and gold – the part of the coast at which Rupert and his men first touched down, south of Cape Blanco in Arguin (in modern Mauritania), was barren and cut off from the richer and more generously watered lands farther south. It was inhabited by lawless Moorish nomads whose sheep and goats provided the only drink, whose arms were darts and lances and who did not take kindly to strangers. But the natural harbour where Rupert found himself was a good one, while ample fish, particularly mullet, was available as fresh food.

Rupert's sailors and soldiers set up their tents on shore while their ships were heeled over and their bottoms scraped and sheathed against worm in preparation for their western journey. A Dutch vessel, which had also taken refuge there, was willing to supply them with planks. Rupert was so pleased with the friendliness of its captain and crew that he hired the ship to carry one of his officers with some of his cargo and letters to the King's ministers in France. The goods that he sent included sugar and ginger; he apologized for their quality, pointing out that his better goods had gone to the bottom with the *Constant Reformation*. Writing to Sir Edward Herbert, the King's attorney-general, he said: 'If His Majesty or the Duke of York be in necessity themselves, pray dispose of all to what they need of, for their own use; I mean after the debts I made at Toulon for the fleet are satisfied.'

Before the ships had been careened Rupert, out of natural curiosity, made an effort to establish contact with the elusive Moors. But they refused to trade with him and preferred to

Opposite In the lower right corner of this engraving of Rupert can just be seen the Moorish child that he unwillingly acquired during his visit to north-west Africa.

Prince Maurice.

decamp, leaving their cattle behind. In an attempt to detain them Rupert shot a camel on which a man, his wife and their child were mounted. The parents managed to mount another camel, but the child was left behind. After vain attempts at negotiations, which resulted only in the killing of one or two of his men, the Prince was left with the child, a boy of about four, who clung to his legs and was subsequently to figure as 'the little nigger' in Rupert's life story much as his dog Boye had done in his younger days.

The cleaned and repaired ships now sailed for the Cape Verde Islands, which belonged to Portugal; the governor of Santiago, to the south-west of the group, made them welcome, promising assistance and supplies. The island, which had a good fortified harbour, was rich in fruit and negroes. The governor added to his good offices by informing Rupert that some English ships were anchored in the Gambia river on the mainland to the south, and offering his pilots as guides. At the end of February 1652 Rupert led his three remaining ships, the *Swallow*, the *Revenge* and the *Honest Seaman*, each armed with forty guns, up the river in search of victims.

Although the pilots managed to run two of the men-of-war aground, the ships were got off without too much difficulty; altogether three English ships and a small Spanish vessel were seized, amounting to a prize of considerable value. Richard Ollard writes in his excellent biography of Rupert's friend and companion, Captain Robert Holmes, that the negroes who had betrayed the hiding place in a creek of one of the English merchant ships 'did not appreciate that Rupert was exercising a lawful authority over rebellious subjects vested in him by his Sacred Majesty King Charles II. Pardonably they had put him down as just another European cut-throat and had darted off up the river to massacre the crew of yet a third small craft. Rupert had it made clear to them that the shedding of Christian blood was not a privilege to be usurped by infidels.

On his way back from the Gambia to the Cape Verde Islands, which he finally reached on 2 March 1652 with his own ships and prizes, he captured another large English vessel and two smaller ones, a valuable haul. But he got into trouble when he stopped at a small seaport to buy provisions and was involved in a skirmish in the surf with African negroes who were handier with their arrows than the sailors were with their muskets. One of the arrows wounded Rupert and he had to cut it out himself. By his bravery, however, he was able to recover two of his sailors who had been taken prisoner. Another mishap was that the sailors on the *Revenge*, who consisted mainly of men taken from prizes, grasped at an opportunity to mutiny, overpowered their officers and sailed home to England, where they related with gusto how Rupert was engaging in piracy, while his few remaining warships were leaking.

In spite of these setbacks the Prince and his brother, bloated with their spoils and amply supplied with water and provisions, were at last ready to venture across the Atlantic. One of the impounded merchantmen was converted into a man-of-war and named the *Defiance*, and Maurice hoisted his flag on it. A final supply of provisions was taken on at Santiago, and Rupert presented the remains of one of his prize ships to a religious community there. Here too a treacherous sailor was shot to ensure discipline. On 9 May the squadron left Santiago and set off for the West Indies.

The journey across the Atlantic in May 1652 can scarcely have been a comfortable one for Rupert's makeshift squadron, even though he had taken immense pains over repairing and provisioning his ships. When it reached a point about 150 miles east of Barbados his flagship the *Swallow* sprung a leak near the stern, which could only be dealt with by baling. So occupied were the officers and men that the leading vessel overshot Barbados on the night of 26 May. But they managed to reach the uninhabited island of St Lucia in the Windward group where, to general satisfaction, they were successful in stopping the leak. The island had ample water, wild hogs, goats and other natural resources. Thus refreshed, the squadron sailed north to Martinique in the Lesser Antilles, which belonged to the French. Though they were received with friendship (the French monarchy had not yet allied with the English Commonwealth), they learned bad news. Ayscue had easily won the race across the Atlantic; the royalists in Barbados had capitulated at the beginning of the year; and Ayscue, satisfied with the island's security, had turned back for home the week before.

What was now to be done? Rupert decided to search the islands for English trading ships, which he could take as prizes.

Turning farther north from Martinique, he sailed past the other large French island, Guadeloupe, stopping at Dominica, where Indians with their faces painted red swapped fruit for glass beads – and reached Montserrat on Whitsunday, 5 June. Here two small English vessels were seized; then they went on to Nevis, where another English prize was captured. Thence Rupert returned to Basse Terre in Guadeloupe, where he vainly tried to persuade the French governor to concert an operation with him against the English islands, which included Antigua, Montserrat and Nevis as well as Barbados. Fearing that the French might now be favouring the Commonwealth, Rupert transferred his squadron to another uninhabited island, this time in the Virgin group.

The harbour in which he careened his ships during June was to be known in future as Cavalier harbour or Rupert's Bay. Here the royalist sailors burned the hulks of three of their prizes, including the *John*, which they had brought all the way from the creeks of West Africa, after transferring their contents onto other ships. Rupert remained there for some time and then the squadron, consisting of four ships, set sail for Anguilla, an island to the south-east.

But the squadron ran into a terrible hurricane blowing from the north. The *Swallow*'s sails were torn down; miraculously it escaped being wrecked on the rocks and finally, with the wind blowing east, was able to shelter safely at another of the Virgin Islands known as St Ann's. However, in the storm all of Rupert's other ships were lost. The *Honest Seaman* was wrecked as far west as Hispaniola, while the *Defiance*, which carried Prince Maurice, was lost with all hands south of Puerto Rico. The diarist of these adventures wrote of the dead prince: 'Many had more power, few more merit: he was snatched from us in obscurity, lest, beholding his loss would have prevented some from endeavouring their own safety: so much he lived beloved, and died bewailed.'

Undoubtedly, if Rupert had felt the slightest hope of finding his brother alive, he would have tried to do so, but he could hardly have doubted his fate in that dreadful hurricane of September 1652. Nothing now remained for him but to return to Europe with his sole warship.

After refitting in Cavalier Harbour, he took a prize, which

he was able to sell in Guadeloupe in return for supplies. Then, having learned that the Dutch and English republics were now at war, he struck up a friendship with the commander of a Dutch ship there, who told him that there were three English merchantmen lying off Antigua. These Rupert promptly seized on 30 October. In November he embarked on his final cruise in the West Indies, during which he captured more prizes and paid a courtesy visit to the Dutch island of St Eustatius, south of the Virgins.

It was on 12 December 1652, with the *Swallow* plus four of the prizes – which he placed under the charge of his friend Robert Holmes – that he embarked on his return voyage across the Atlantic. This time he received no comfort from the Portuguese (whose government was looking for an alliance with the Commonwealth) in any of the islands of the Azores, where his crews met with nothing but bullets and foul weather. Yet the old weather-beaten *Swallow* (it had been built nineteen years earlier) ended its long adventures without serious mishap. On 3 March 1653 Rupert sighted Belle Îsle off the coast of Brittany, where he hove to before it was dark and the moon eclipsed. Next day the *Swallow* entered the Loire to anchor at St Nazaire not far from Nantes. Rupert's journey from Kinsale to Lisbon, into the Mediterranean and on to West Africa, the Caribbean and back had taken some thirty months and must have covered about 7,000 miles. It was an heroic episode.

⚜   ⚜   ⚜

Historians have often dismissed Rupert as having been a mere pirate chief; certainly that is how his enemies in England regarded him. But it has to be remembered that when the Prince sailed from Ireland to Portugal not a single government in Europe had recognized the Free Commonwealth as legitimate, while every monarch had been thunderstruck by the public execution of Charles I. Indeed it was not until the end of 1650 that the Spaniards, hoping to steal a march on the French, did so. Rupert had been welcomed by King John IV of Portugal as the admiral appointed by a hereditary king. In fact, except in the case of the Spaniards after the act of recognition, Rupert had been scrupulous – or at any rate fairly scrupulous – not to impound the ships of friendly powers such as the French and the Dutch. He had, it is true, once laid hold of a Genoese vessel as a reprisal; on the other hand, he had released a Danish ship taken by his men.

Secondly, it must be noted how skilful and courageous Rupert proved himself to be as an admiral. Sir John Mennes, his most experienced officer, who had been his rear-admiral in Ireland, left the squadron before it sailed for Portugal. Captain Thomas Allin, who had once commanded his frigates, was taken prisoner off the Scillies at an early stage. Captain Craven was lost in the Caribbean. Only Captain Fearnes, who had considerable knowledge of the sea, stayed with him throughout the whole adventure, but Fearnes, a crusty professional, was neither respected by his officers nor trusted by his men; indeed he seems to have been out for loot rather than moved by any sense of loyalty to the royal cause.

Rupert quickly mastered the arts of seamanship. Had he not done so, he could scarcely have survived the buffetings of the Atlantic storms nor coped with the other misfortunes that lined his way. According to the diarist of the voyage, even at the very end it was his dexterity in trimming the *Swallow* that prevented it from being wrecked in the Loire. More important even than his technical skill were his gifts of leadership and diplomacy. Had it not been for those, he could not have overcome the savages of Africa, the Indians in the Caribbean or the doubts of Portuguese and French governors.

What had he accomplished? It might be said, very little. Yet, as the famous American naval historian Captain Mahan pointed out many years ago, the weaker power at sea has no alternative but to engage in commerce destroying. And Rupert never possessed the means, even though he was willing to take his chances, to fight a set battle against men like Popham and Blake who not only had newer ships but also better trained crews. It can reasonably be contended that if Rupert had reached Barbados ahead of Ayscue he might have shown himself an able amphibian by resuming the profession of soldier and building up the defences of the island so that they became impregnable. It is hard to measure the necessity for his delays – particularly in West Africa – but it is likely that without them he would never have been able to cross the Atlantic at all. What he did, then, was to keep the royalist standard flying in distant seas and far-flung islands. His name brought not only fear to his enemies but comfort to his friends. He did what he could to acquire goods and send help to the King in exile; had it not been for the sinking of all but one of his warships, he might have brought back succour sufficient to help Charles II to regain his lost throne. As it was, so long as one heroic admiral was willing to risk his life in the cause, King Charles, his exiled court and his adherents lying low in England could hope that one day they would be victorious.

Chapter Nine

✤

ADMIRAL AGAIN

Before Rupert left the Loire, he showed his skill in seamanship by taking the *Swallow* safely along the river to Paimboeuf, a port higher up than St Nazaire, after it had been run aground by a local pilot. Rupert then left Robert Holmes in charge of the ships and cargoes: his task was to pay off the sailors, make out inventories, and strip the smaller ships of their masts and guns. Rupert himself intended to join Charles II and his court in Paris, travelling by land via Nantes. But at Nantes he was taken seriously ill, which was scarcely surprising considering his adventures at sea, the poor quality of the food, the depression caused by the death of his brother and the loss of his valuable cargoes purchased at so high a price. King Charles II at once sent a messenger to him, with a letter expressing his impatience to see him again as quickly as his health would permit. By April 1653 Rupert had reached the Palais Royale, where he was welcomed not only by his royal cousin but by King Louis XIV of France, a lively lad of fourteen who was excited to hear about the wanderer's astonishing exploits.

For some time Rupert remained out of sorts and stayed indoors. But by May he was writing to Holmes asking him to send along a few of his treasures, including ivory and chocolate and 'the little nigger' he had brought with him all the way from West Africa. There were also three blackamoor servants, and parrots and monkeys. But most of the cargo, including ginger, cinnamon, indigo and copper bars, and ivory and sugar as well as guns and riggings from the prizes, were sold for what they would fetch. After Holmes had completed his inventories – not without obstruction from two or three hardened professional officers accustomed to embezzling, and from the demobilized crews who wanted their money – Rupert returned to Nantes to supervise the sales. The Commonwealth government had officially protested to the court of France that the goods seized from the prizes rightfully belonged to it, but the French put no difficulties in Rupert's way. He also aimed to dispose of the *Swallow* and its brass guns, after receiving an authorization from Charles II to do so. The *Swallow*, however, appears to have sunk when sent out of the river to a neighbouring port for repair: 'like a grateful servant,' in the romantic words of the diarist, 'having brought her master through so many dangers, she consumed herself, scorning after being quitted by him that any inferior person should command her.'

Now a squabble arose over the money raised by the sales. The King was extremely hard up at the time, as the French government had withheld a promised pension and his mother was mean with her help. Charles naturally hoped that Rupert would be in a position to tide him over his stringency. But Rupert firmly said that the first call on the money must be the pay of the sailors and the reimbursement of the debts he had contracted at Toulon before he left France. Hyde, the King's Chancellor of the Exchequer, was highly indignant, claiming that there was no proper accounting, while Rupert's friend, Sir Edward Herbert, the Lord Keeper, sided with the Prince. One of Rupert's brothers wrote to his sister: 'To tell you which is right [the King or Rupert] would be a difficult thing for me to judge. I think they are both wrong, since each has his idiot who governs him and the two idiots hate each other like the plague.' Pretty reliable evidence exists, however, that Rupert did let the King have some money, that he took nothing for himself, and that the debts at Toulon remained unpaid, at any rate until after Charles II's restoration.

In the early summer of 1654 the quarrel was made up. Rupert was a quick-tempered man but Charles was as a rule easy-going. Rupert left Paris first for Heidelberg, then for Vienna. By the Peace of Westphalia, signed in 1648, Rupert's eldest brother, Charles Louis, was restored to the Lower Palatinate and to the title of elector, while Rupert was promised 30,000 rix-dollars, a sizable sum in modern money, as part of the compensation for the loss of the Upper Palatinate. The Elector had a hard task in establishing his rule over the duchy from which he had been in exile for thirty years, and which had been fought over and desolated, so he had trouble in providing a suitable estate for his brother, while a complicated rivalry for the affections of a beautiful girl stirred up jealousy.

Rupert then went on to Vienna, where he received more of a welcome, since he had struck up a friendship with the Emperor Ferdinand III when, years earlier, he had been released from his imprisonment in Linz. The Emperor acknowledged his financial obligation (the 30,000 rix-dollars), but unfortunately was unable to find the capital sum then and there to meet it; in the meantime he promised yearly instalments plus interest on the capital. After returning during the winter to Heidelberg, where his elder brother evidently hinted that he had best find himself military employment, Rupert rejoined Charles II, who had been politely thrown out of France by Mazarin because the Cardinal was busily engaged in concluding a treaty with the Commonwealth. The King, being wanted neither in France nor in the Netherlands, had set up his court at Cologne. Loyalty to the exiled Stuarts was still at the top of Rupert's priorities. Though he was offered one or two military missions, for example by the Duke of Modena, he always stood ready to serve Charles II.

It seems that one idea being considered at this time was that Rupert should go to Scotland to try to revive the royalist cause there. It was perhaps hoped that he would prove another Montrose, who, after brilliant campaigning, had finally been defeated and executed at Edinburgh in May 1650. The dour and capable General George Monck had recently resumed his military governorship of Scotland, while abortive royalist risings had been put down. But it was intimated – though obscurely – that Rupert would not be a *persona grata* with the Scots because of his swashbuckling reputation – which was a little odd because he had been born and bred a Calvinist. Nor was Rupert enthusiastic about Charles II's attempts to obtain assistance from the Spaniards, who were about to declare war on the Commonwealth; Rupert had never forgiven them for the way they had treated him in the winter of 1649, and therefore distrusted them.

For a time Rupert returned to Heidelberg and resumed friendly relations with his brother: this was in the summer and autumn of 1655. But when Rupert, after paying another visit to Vienna, tried to return to Heidelberg a year later the Elector, who was still desperately hard up, sent strict orders from his hunting lodge that Rupert was not to be allowed into the castle, which had been shut up, including the kitchens. So Rupert had no home and precious little money. His parrots and monkeys were dead and he even had to give away his little nigger, who died in the cold of Brandenburg, far away from his West African birthplace. Rupert had no heart to resume his military career as a mercenary captain. He divided his next four years between Frankfurt on Main, the imperial free city where he held an honorific appointment given him by the Emperor, and Hesse Cassel and Mainz where the rulers were his friends.

During these years Rupert amused himself by experimenting in the laboratory: he aimed to improve the quality of gunpowder, and he devised a rudimentary revolver and a primitive torpedo. He also contrived what came to be known as 'Prince Rupert's drops' which were 'pear-shaped drops of glass, unbreakable at their thick end, and ... constructed by putting refined and melted green glass into cold water'. More valuable was his discovery of the method of engraving known as mezzotint. Rupert claimed, at any rate, that he was the inventor and John Evelyn, a connoisseur in such matters, wrote in his book *Sculptura* (1662) that he was, though it is generally asserted that the process was invented by an obscure German colonel who disclosed the secret to Rupert. It is by no means clear why Rupert should have lied on such a question nor is it of much importance. What is certain is that Rupert executed some extremely fine mezzotints, including 'the head of the Great Executioner' or 'the executioner of St John', which is in the British Museum, and two of his famous enemy, Oliver Cromwell, which are in the Ashmolean.

In May 1660 Charles II, partly owing to the exertions of General Monck, who marched from Scotland to Westminster, and partly in accordance with the wishes of many of his subjects, who were tiring of anarchy, was restored to his throne. Rupert, having no real home – for his brother had made it plain that he was not wanted in Heidelberg – was invited by his cousin to England. Samuel Pepys, just beginning his long career as a naval administrator, for some reason took a dislike to Rupert

King Charles II – a medal commemorating his
Restoration in 1660.

and wrote on 29 September 1660 that 'Prince Rupert is come to Court welcome to nobody'.

After staying for six months the Prince went to visit his mother, who was now sixty-five, at The Hague. As he no longer had his dog or his black boy, he brought his greyhounds and beagles with him. Next he went to Brandenburg where he heard rumours of a coming war against the Turks; had he been offered a command, he said, it would have attracted him. Moving on to Vienna, where the youthful Leopold I had succeeded his father Ferdinand III in 1657, he had a lukewarm reception. It is true that the Holy Roman Emperor borrowed his greyhounds for a hunt and that he was considered for the command of the imperial cavalry. But the offer fell through because he was 'not a Roman' and senior German officers felt they had a better right to the post. So he returned to England at the beginning of 1662 to settle in London. He was now forty-two.

After his arrival Charles II appointed Rupert a member of his Privy Council and asked him to serve on the committee

157

Rupert's mezzotint portrait of his old adversary, Oliver Cromwell.

which dealt with the affairs of Tangier, formerly a Portuguese possession, which had been part of the dowry of the King's young wife, Catherine of Braganza. Rupert became a shareholder in the Royal African Company of which James Duke of York was president. He was an active member of the recently formed Royal Society, and had his own laboratory in the palace of Whitehall, where he carried out experiments. He had his old friends: Robert Holmes, who had accompanied him throughout the long sea voyage, Will Legge, who had been so loyal to him in Oxford, and others of the older Cavaliers. Though still a bachelor, he showed himself not indifferent to the ladies of a court which had thrown off Puritan inhibitions.

His chance to resume service at sea arose when a war against the United Netherlands came into the offing. Antagonism between the Dutch and the English had first flared up in 1651 when quarrels over precedence at sea and colonial questions had led to the First Anglo–Dutch War, which was won when Cromwell was Lord Protector. The treaty concluding the war was humiliating to the Dutch, while the causes of rivalry remained. Rupert himself did not at first think highly of the Dutch as warriors. In May when he was in Brandenburg he had written to Legge, 'the Hollanders boast much avowing openly that if the King doth trouble the herring fishing, they will maintain it with the sword', but Rupert despised the butter and cheese merchants. He was to learn his error. The King had no wish to go to war, but his parliament, elected in 1661, was ready to do so and soon events pressed in that direction.

At the beginning of 1664 Robert Holmes was sent on a mission on behalf of the Royal African Company to the west coast of Africa. When he reached the Cape Verde Islands, where he had last been with Rupert, he started taking Dutch prizes and occupied Goree Island, a Dutch trading post. Then moving farther south he captured more Dutch ships and all the trading posts in Sierra Leone, the Ivory Coast and the Gold Coast. By the autumn he was back in Europe, though he did not reach Portsmouth until mid-December. Meanwhile the Duke of York had sent another freebooting captain, Richard Nicolls, to occupy New Amsterdam (the future city of New York) on the ground that the English settlement on Long Island had been annoyed by the Dutch in Manhattan.

Naturally enough, the government of the United Netherlands was extremely indignant. By October 1664 it dispatched its finest admiral, Michael de Ruyter, to West Africa where he retook Goree and all the other posts occupied by Holmes except for one. In reply to Dutch protests Charles II committed Holmes to imprisonment in the Tower of London, but he did not lack creature comforts there. At the same time that Nicolls was capturing New Amsterdam Rupert, with his first-rate knowledge of the West African coast, volunteered to lead a fleet there against de Ruyter and was put in command of a small

Michael de Ruyter, the finest Dutch admiral of his time, swiftly retaliated against English encroachments upon his country's strongholds in West Africa.

and ill-equipped expeditionary force intended for Guinea. However Rupert was taken ill, for the head wound he had received in 1647 re-opened. The Duke of York sent his surgeon to attend to him, but though the surgeon operated it did not do Rupert much good – he always distrusted doctors – and the expedition was called off.

On 22 February, following an attempt by an English admiral to capture a Dutch mercantile fleet returning from Smyrna, a full-scale conflict, to be known as the Second Anglo–Dutch War, began. Both sides had a formidable fleet consisting of about a hundred men-of-war and auxiliary ships. The Duke of York, who was Lord High Admiral at the age of thirty-two, held the supreme command. Rupert, whose previous naval experience had been as a leader of a small squadron, was appointed admiral of the White (or van) with Holmes serving as one of his captains; the Earl of Sandwich commanded the Blue (or rear) while the Duke of York led the Red (or centre). Within each of these three squadrons which made up the royal fleet there was a vice-admiral who was in charge of the van and a rear-admiral of the rear. When the signal to engage was given each squadron was required to follow one of the three admirals on a line bearing parallel to that of the enemy. This system, known as 'line ahead', had been introduced by Monck and Blake when they were generals-at-sea in the First Anglo–Dutch War. Indeed the royal fleet contained a considerable number of officers who had been Roundheads, including the Earl of Sandwich (as Edward Montagu he had been in command of the Commonwealth navy at the time of the Restoration), and Sir George Ayscue, who had beaten Rupert in the race to Barbados.

In April the fleet anchored at the Gunfleet near the mouth of the Thames and then cruised off the Dutch coast aiming to intercept enemy convoys arriving at the Texel and thus provoke the Dutch navy to come out to fight in their defence. Rupert himself was sceptical of the wisdom of this strategy and indeed after less than three weeks at sea the English ships were forced back to the Gunfleet owing to lack of supplies. However, on 30 May Rupert learned that the Dutch, under the command of Jacob van Wassenaer Lord of Obdam, with a slightly bigger and better fleet, were moving north to Southwold Bay in Suffolk eager for a fight.

On 2 June the wind veered from east-north-east to east-south-east so that Rupert was able to gain the weather gauge over the approaching Dutchmen. The battle began fourteen miles south-east of Lowestoft early in the morning of 3 June; each side endeavoured to maintain line ahead; twice two lines of ships filed past each other. Rupert tacked as soon as the Dutch passed the first time, although the sails and hull of the *Royal James* were much torn already. According to the journal of the Earl of Sandwich, Rupert showed superb seamanship by timely tacking and 'kept his luff', that is to say brought the ship's bow nearer the wind. So the two lines sailed past each other a second time on opposite tacks; but comparatively little

161

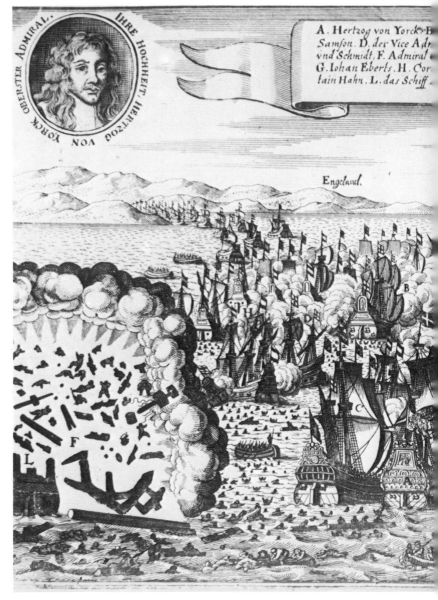

The battle of
Lowestoft, 3 June 1665.

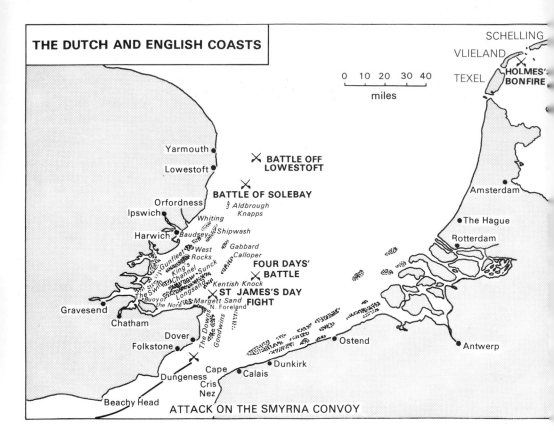

THE DUTCH AND ENGLISH COASTS

0 10 20 30 40
miles

SCHELLING
VLIELAND
TEXEL
HOLMES'S BONFIRE

Yarmouth
Lowestoft
BATTLE OFF LOWESTOFT
BATTLE OF SOLEBAY
Orfordness
Ipswich
Aldbrough
Knapps
Whiting
Harwich
Baudsey
Shipwash
West Rocks
Gabbard
Calloper
FOUR DAYS' BATTLE
Gunfleet
King's
Channel
Sunck
Longsand
Kentish Knock
ST JAMES'S DAY FIGHT
The Buoy of the Nore
Margett Sand
N. Foreland
Gravesend
Chatham
The Downs
Goodwins
Dover
Folkstone
Ostend
Dungeness
Cape Cris Nez
Calais
Dunkirk
Antwerp
Beachy Head
Amsterdam
The Hague
Rotterdam
ATTACK ON THE SMYRNA CONVOY

damage was done by the broadsides in which the Dutch fired at the English masts and rigging and the English at the Dutch hulls. As noon approached the battle developed into a hot and confused dog-fight.

The White squadron was nearly always in the van and Rupert was said to have been 'the boldest attacker in the world for personal courage'. About one or two o'clock Obdam's flag-ship suddenly blew up; the Dutch admiral and some 400 of the crew were killed or drowned. This signified a complete victory for the English. But owing to some kind of muddle on the Duke of York's flagship when James himself was asleep, orders were given to shorten sail so that the chase was called off. Each side returned to its home port. In London bonfires were lit, bells were rung and there was general rejoicing.

A month after the victory off Lowestoft the Duke of York and Prince Rupert left the fleet in the company of the King on board a pleasure boat bound for London. Charles II did not want to risk their lives again, as at the Battle of Lowestoft, so he promoted the Earl of Sandwich to be sole admiral. Sandwich blotted his copybook first by failing to intercept a Dutch convoy at Bergen in Denmark and secondly, when at the end of August he did manage to capture nine Dutch East Indiamen as prizes, by promptly dividing the booty with his officers without the permission of the Lord High Admiral. Consequently he was removed from his command and in the following year Rupert and Monck, now Duke of Albemarle, were put in joint charge of the fleet. It was said that 'the two Generals governed with that Unity and Agreement as if they had been acted by one soul'.

When campaigning was resumed in the spring of 1666, the French reluctantly agreed to fulfil their obligations incurred under the terms of a defensive alliance with the Dutch concluded four years earlier. The Duke of Beaufort left Toulon on 29 April with a French squadron, but it was feared that an English squadron which had been in the Mediterranean might return and attack him so he was ordered to shelter in the Tagus. While he was still there the English Admiralty received completely false intelligence that he had reached Brest and was about to make for the eastern end of the English Channel. So on 25 May the Duke of York ordered that the fleet, then stationed off the South Foreland (whence it had been removed from the Nore) should be divided. Rupert, with the *Royal James* and nineteen other warships, was instructed to intercept Beaufort and then hasten to rejoin the main body of the fleet under Albemarle, which was thus depleted to under sixty ships. (The total strength of the navy had also been reduced because many sailors had died in the Great Plague, which had devastated England the year before.) Rupert sailed from the Downs into the Channel on 29 May. Next day Albemarle learned positively that the Dutch fleet had put to sea; despite his inferiority in numbers he prepared to fight. A battle began on 1 June twenty miles off Ostend. Meanwhile Rupert was far away with his twenty warships and a number of fireships, a detached makeshift force engaged on a fool's errand.

Being to windward and having a fair wind, Albemarle determined to attack the Dutch early in the morning of 1 June. But

The English warship, the *Royal Charles*, being carried off by the Dutch after their successful raid on the Medway where the Chatham dockyards lay. (p. 173)

167

then the wind blew so heavily that he was unable to bring his lowest tier of guns into action and eventually was caught between two lines of fire, suffering severe damage to his vessels. On the following day the battle was resumed, but as Albemarle was now reduced to little more than forty ships against nearly eighty Dutch he resolved to draw off towards the English coast, where the Dutch followed him. On the morning of 3 June neither side was able to make much headway, owing to a calm. In the afternoon Prince Rupert, having received a delayed message to rejoin Albemarle, arrived off the treacherous Galloper sands; the Dutch, who were north of the Galloper, hoped to entice Rupert's squadron onto the sands, but Albemarle took the precaution of sending him a warning. That evening the two admirals conferred aboard the *Royal James*. Since Rupert's return the English fleet was little inferior to that of the Dutch; they therefore decided to fall upon the enemy the following day.

As Rupert's ships were fresh, he led the van when fighting was resumed at about eight o'clock on the morning of 4 June. Five times the fleets passed each other firing their broadsides. After about two hours' fighting the Dutch stood off to the north-east but now (according to Michael Lewis's analysis) 'a sight unique till then in sailing ship warfare was seen, the English beating up the wind and breaking through the enemy's line from leeward'. The ships that thus penetrated the Dutch line were led by Rupert's vice-admiral who was killed in the action. The Dutch admiral de Ruyter retorted by keeping his fleet in two lines and concentrating his fire on the two first-rate flagships, the *Royal James* (Rupert's ship, which was partly dismasted) and the *Royal Charles* with Albemarle on board. Though Rupert put up a magnificent fight, the Dutch had the best of the Four Days' battle, as it was called. Albemarle complained that he had never fought with worse captains, only some twenty ships sticking with him during the battle. Of Rupert it was said that he did 'manifest a courage and conduct answerable to the other great actions which belong to the story of his life whereby he gave spirit to his friends and terror to the enemy'.

Rupert's own views about the reasons why the English navy did not do better in the battle of the Four Days were set out in some detail in a narrative which he prepared for the House of Commons when the campaigning season ended. He complained about faulty intelligence, first in regard to the movements of the French squadron which he had been sent to intercept, secondly about the time when the Dutch were expected to come out of their harbours; and he protested over the delay in his receiving news of Albemarle's whereabouts after he was at last instructed to rejoin him. He also spoke of 'intolerable neglect' in supplying adequate provisions throughout the campaign, particularly beer; of 'the want of seamen ... too great to be forgotten'; and finally of 'the horrible neglects' in the shipyards. No wonder the indefatigable Pepys and the Navy Board were not fond of Rupert.

Although the English suffered heavy casualties and lost ten ships in this battle, both sides recovered quickly. De Ruyter was again at sea on 26 June, but owing to unfavourable weather and lack of competent pilots he had to wait for the English to come out of the Thames. The two fleets sighted each other on 24 July and a battle took place next day thirty-six miles southeast of Orfordness in Suffolk. The fight resolved itself into direct contests between the three squadrons, which made up a total of eighty ships on each side. Rupert and Albemarle were together this time on board the *Royal Charles* in the centre. The struggle between the two vans and two centres went in favour of the English, but the rear or Blue squadron under Sir Jeremy Smith was outmanoeuvred by the Dutch commanded by Cornelis van Tromp, son of the famous Maarten van Tromp who was killed in 1653. Although the battle, to be known as St James's Fight, was a victory for the English, the Dutch lost only two ships and the English one. Rupert's friend Robert Holmes, who served in the Blue squadron, blamed Smith for allowing Tromp's squadron to escape.

Twelve days later Holmes distinguished himself. Rupert and Albemarle, acting on the basis of information supplied by a Dutch traitor, ordered him to raid the islands of Vlie and Schelling off the Zuider Zee with a task force consisting of two thirds soldiers and one third sailors. His ships were frigates, but he also had five fireships and seven ketches. Holmes entered the channel between the islands on 9 August, when he decided of his own accord to send in his fireships. He claimed to have burned some 150 Dutch merchantmen at anchor there without

'A Representation of the English Royall Navy under the Command of his H Prince Rupert and the Duke of Albemarle riding before Vly at the burning of above 150 Dutch vessels and the Towne of Skelling wch service was performed under the conduct of Sr Robert Holmes.'

losing a ship himself and sustaining only a dozen casualties. The cost to the Dutch from what came to be known as 'Holmes's bonfire' was £1 million.

Though the rival fleets were at sea again in the autumn no major contest took place. Albemarle was recalled to London to take charge after the Great Fire which broke out early in September. Rupert was therefore left in sole charge of the navy. He told Albemarle on 11 September that his intention was to

sail towards the enemy as soon as the weather cleared, but in fact both fleets were handicapped by strong gales. However, Rupert had the satisfaction of learning that Dutch ships mistook one of his for a Frenchman, and when giving chase to it were forced ashore on the French coast and destroyed.

Samuel Pepys, Clerk of the Acts to the Navy Board, who considered that Rupert was bad-tempered and obstinate, had the temerity to complain to King Charles II that the Prince had

Cornelis van Tromp.

brought back the fleet in a poor condition from the campaign of 1666. At a meeting on 7 October Rupert 'rose up and told the King that whatever the gentleman [Pepys] said, he had brought home his fleet in as good a condition as ever any fleet was brought home'. Albemarle seconded him, so that was that.

During the following winter Rupert was seriously ill; another two trepanning operations had to be performed on his old head wound. For that reason he can scarcely have been consulted by

172

the King over the decisions taken early in 1667 about the use of the navy. Negotiations for peace with the Dutch had been opened, so the King and the majority of his Privy Council resolved – partly because of the exhausted state of the royal finances – to lay up the larger warships while maintaining a squadron of frigates to destroy as much Dutch commerce as possible. So seamen were laid off and ships docked at Chatham and elsewhere to undergo repair. Rupert protested when he heard of this intention.

Rupert had also warned the King the previous October to fortify Harwich, the nearest port to Holland, and Sheerness on the Isle of Sheppey, which guarded the entrance to the Thames, in case the Dutch attempted to attack them. Charles did in fact visit Sheerness twice himself and gave orders for the fortification of the two vulnerable positions. Nevertheless the Dutch government, which had kept its fleet in being, determined to sanction a bold raid on England as well as a diversion against Scotland. Admiral Michael de Ruyter was dispatched in command of a task force of fifty or sixty ships with the aim of raiding the Thames and the Medway, the tributary which led to the Chatham dockyard. Early in June Sheerness fort was captured; then while de Ruyter himself, with most of his fleet, stayed as a covering force at the mouth of the Thames he sent Lieutenant-Admiral Willem van Ghent into the Medway. Van Ghent broke through the defences that guarded Chatham dockyard, set six English warships on fire, and got away safely with the *Royal Charles*, the Duke of York's flagship, and a frigate, the *Unity*, which he brought down the Thames, across the North Sea and home to Holland.

The importance of this sensational raid has sometimes been exaggerated. As soon as intelligence of the coming of the Dutch fleet was received at Whitehall the Duke of Albemarle dashed to Chatham while Rupert was ordered to Woolwich. But Albemarle arrived too late to inflict serious damage on the Dutch, who were hailed as heroes when they reached home. In a statement which he wrote for the information of the House of Commons Rupert blamed the *débâcle* on the failure to fortify Sheerness sufficiently, 'to which neglect we may justly ascribe the burning of the ships at Chatham, and the dishonour that attended it. Last of all,' he added, 'I do esteem it none of the

The raid on the
Medway, from a
contemporary Dutch
print.

175

least miscarriages that have been observable in the last war that no fleet was kept in a body last summer, especially since the enemy was known to be arming; whereas we had above 18,000 seamen all the while in pay upon the dispersed ships which if but a part had been kept together in the Thames, it had probably have been the prevention of the mischief that ensued.'

Who precisely was to blame for allowing the Dutch raid is even now not clear. The Duke of York as Lord High Admiral, whose ultimate responsibility it was, had been opposed – like Rupert and Albemarle – to the decision to lay up the big ships instead of keeping an adequate fleet to guard the approaches from Holland across the North Sea. Lord Arlington, one of the secretaries of state, was a keen advocate of economizing at the expense of the navy, while Sir William Coventry, who was soon to be appointed a treasury commissioner, had told Pepys flatly that it was 'impossible' to send out another fleet in the spring of 1667. Charles II himself approved the policy of retrenchment because he was tired of the war and wanted to conclude a treaty with the French, who were the allies of the Dutch.

After reading Rupert's statement the House of Commons passed a vote of confidence in him and Albemarle, thanking them 'for their care and conduct in the last year's war'. Just three years later Albemarle died. It was a tribute to Rupert's honourable reputation at sea that after the Third Anglo–Dutch War began in 1672 he was appointed sole commander of the English navy.

Chapter Ten

❧

THE LAST BATTLE

The war with the Dutch that began in March 1672 had a rather different background from that of the previous naval war. King Charles II was now enthusiastic: he had obtained the alliance with the French that he craved; he was seeking revenge for the humiliations inflicted upon him in 1667; and the secret treaty between the two crowns, concluded at Dover in May 1670, provided that after the French army and English navy had won their expected victory over the cheese merchants the United Netherlands were to be divided into three parts. The French would extend their frontiers; the English would gain valuable ports to the east of the North Sea; and the truncated remains of the republic would be ruled as a kingdom by Charles's nephew, Prince William III of Orange. Events did not in fact work out that way. William, though only twenty-one, was appointed Captain-General and Admiral-General of the United Netherlands and resolved to fight to the death against Anglo–French aggression.

James Duke of York, as Lord High Admiral, again took personal charge of the English fleet and was in command of the Red (centre) squadron, to which the French fleet under Vice-Admiral Jean d'Estrées was joined as the White (van) squadron; the Earl of Sandwich, who had been kicked upstairs during the previous war by being sent as ambassador to Spain, was recalled to take command of the Blue (rear) squadron. The objective was to effect a landing on the Dutch coast in support of a direct assault on Holland by the French army. A short, sharp war was anticipated—indeed Charles II had had difficulty in raising enough funds to fight even one campaign at sea. The Dutch, for their part, adopted a defensive–offensive strategy. In fact the first battle of the war was fought off South-wold Bay. It was fiercely contested and cost heavy casualties on both sides; van Ghent, the hero of the raid on the Medway, was killed and Sandwich was drowned. The Dutch achieved their aim of discouraging the English from a direct attack on their coasts. Moreover the failure of d'Estrées's squadron, which played a minor part in the battle, made the French un-popular both at Whitehall and Westminster.

Rupert did not serve at sea in this campaign, but was placed in charge of the home defences. He then irritated the Navy Board by closely interesting himself in the supplies for the fleet. Naturally, since he had complained about the administrative side of the navy at the close of the campaign of 1666, he was anxious to discover for himself where the responsibility lay. No doubt he learned that although there was the usual peculation among seventeenth-century civil servants, the ultimate blame for deficiencies could be placed on the Commons who kept the King short of money.

After the Battle of Southwold Bay stalemate developed at sea, but the French were victorious on land, so the Dutch were anxious for peace. This left Charles II optimistic. In February 1673 he asked the House of Commons for money to continue the war. The Commons hesitated: they felt incensed because during the recess the King, without consulting them, had published a declaration of religious indulgence, which was regarded as unconstitutional and as a sop to the English Roman Catholics and to King Louis XIV of France. In return for his withdrawing the declaration and for giving the royal assent to a Test Act, which excluded all who were not members of the Church of England from holding office, the Commons voted a grant to the King of £70,000 a month for eighteen months, about sufficient to carry on the naval war for another year.

Though the Duke of York had not yet openly declared him-self to be a Roman Catholic, he was one in fact and felt obliged to resign as Lord High Admiral. The Admiralty was placed in the hands of a commission, and Rupert was given the com-mand at sea but without the powers enjoyed by his predecessor. For example, he was not allowed to appoint his own officers. He had asked for Sir Robert Holmes (he had been knighted in 1666 for his services at sea) as his rear-admiral, but was refused.

In the middle of May 1673 the French fleet under d'Estrées joined up with Rupert. Though d'Estrées continued in charge of the White squadron, some of his ships were attached to the English Red and Blue squadrons. Rupert had numerical superiority over the Dutch. His instructions were to defeat de Ruyter so as to prepare the way for a landing in the Dutch rear. Rupert sailed directly east towards the mouth of the Scheldt, hoping to tempt the enemy warships to move out into the open sea from among their islands and shoals. To achieve this purpose he sent forward a task force consisting of frigates and fireships.

In fact de Ruyter came out much sooner than was expected, and a somewhat confused battle followed. The wind was blowing south-south-west and Rupert had the weather gauge. But partly because of the intermingling of the French squadron with his own fleet his line was not properly formed, and he had also to be careful to prevent his vessels running on to the shoals. Two Dutch ships were destroyed in the battle and there were substantial casualties on both sides. The battle was resumed a week later. These contests became known as the First and Second Battles of Schoonveldt. This time the wind was northeast, giving the Dutch an advantage. Again the battle was drawn, but the Dutch had proved themselves fully capable of protecting their own coasts.

Rupert blamed his lack of success in these two battles on the navy commissioners for not allowing his ships sufficient supplies. He insisted that he would not serve again unless given fuller powers. On 9 July his demand was met. Not only was he appointed general and commander-in-chief on land and sea, but he was created First Commissioner of the Admiralty.

Nevertheless his instructions were dictated to him. In the middle of July Pepys took down the resolutions of the council of flag-officers. Rupert was ordered to undertake a defensive–offensive strategy in preparation for an army landing on the Dutch coast to be commanded by a former Marshal of France whom Charles II had hired for the purpose, the German Frederick Herman Count of Schömberg.

However, when Rupert sailed to the Texel in the second half of July he refused to have his fleet slowed down by escorting

troop transports. The intended landing force was therefore left
behind at Yarmouth. The Anglo–French and Dutch fleets
sighted each other on 10 August. Though the wind was in his
favour Rupert, because it was late in the afternoon, decided
to delay his attack until the next day. The wind veered east
by south during the night and the Dutch obtained the weather
gauge. Rupert sent the French – who, after the confusion off
Schoonveldt, again constituted the White squadron – south to
deal with the enemy from the windward side, hoping to catch
the Dutch between two lines of fire.

Sir Edward Spragge (preferred to Holmes) in charge of the

The inconclusive Battle of the Texel (August 1673) was the last battle of the Anglo–Dutch wars as well as Rupert's last.

Blue fought the Dutch rear under the intrepid Cornelis van Tromp, while Rupert with the Red confronted de Ruyter, who bore down on him with the wind. De Ruyter managed to win local superiority over Rupert, partly because the Dutch van with a smaller number of ships (variously estimated from eight to nineteen) proved capable of coping with some thirty French warships. Spragge and Tromp fought a desperate battle in which Spragge himself was killed. But Rupert succeeded in joining the Blue squadron, although it had been badly mauled.

It was a skilful contest on both sides, in which Rupert used his fireships effectively. Again few ships were lost; in terms of

181

casualties it was a draw. But once again the Dutch, with inferior numbers, had held their own. The English government had to abandon the idea of landing troops in Holland. In February of the following year peace was concluded at Westminster on not unfavourable terms for the English; the French were left to fight on their own against a growing European coalition.

Rupert was naturally disappointed with the result of his last battle, complaining that 'it was the plainest and greatest opportunity lost at sea'. It has been customary for English historians, following Rupert's outspoken opinions, to accuse the French of being culpable. But the battle is fully documented, and an impartial examination suggests that the failure of the French was exaggerated. Rupert had given d'Estrées a formidable task in requiring him to penetrate the Dutch vessels from the leeward to gain the weather gauge. D'Estrées did in fact achieve this, but the Dutch vice-admiral Banckers, a much more skilful sailor (d'Estrées was a soldier and a gentleman, not a professional naval officer), counter-attacked, breaking through the French to rejoin de Ruyter. D'Estrées got separated from some of his other ships and was confused by Rupert's signals from a distance in a battle which began in fog and ended at dusk. The French had fought bravely enough at the earlier battles at Schoonveldt. The supposition that d'Estrées was a coward or that he had been ordered by Louis XIV not to risk his ships unduly has little basis in fact.

Because of Rupert's criticisms the French Minister of Marine investigated the matter thoroughly and was convinced that d'Estrées had done his best – though it might not have been very good. The defeat, if that is what it may be called, did not injure Rupert's high reputation. When he returned to London he received a rapturous greeting from the populace, while his laying the responsibility for lack of complete success on the French was in tune with the mood of the day.

❧   ❧   ❧

Looking back on Rupert's career as a naval commander, one can appreciate that it was by no means negligible. By the time he returned from his trip across the Atlantic he had become

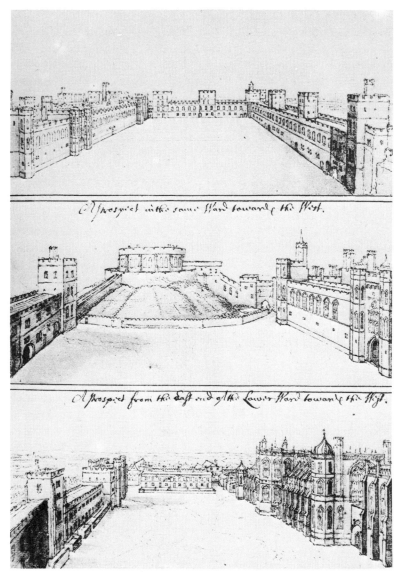

A prospect in the same Ward towards the West.

A prospect from the East end of the Lower Ward towards the West.

Windsor Castle of which Rupert was constable.

an expert in seamanship. As fighting men he and George Monck, Duke of Albemarle, were as rugged a pair as Blake and Monck when he was younger had been during the first war against the Dutch. Tactically Rupert combined the idea of an ordered approach to a battle with an aggressive policy once

183

he came to grips with the enemy. By the time of the Second Anglo–Dutch War the approach known as 'line ahead', which has already been described, had become the standard English practice. It is true that a rough-and-ready follow-my-leader procedure had been adopted by the Royal Navy during the reign of Queen Elizabeth I, but it was not until the reign of Charles II that it became regularly included in the navy's fighting instructions. The aim of the new discipline, in theory at least, was that once the signal from the admiral had been received the ships should space themselves out behind him at hundred-yard intervals so that they could fire their broadsides in orderly fashion. To maintain regular stations they sailed in close-hauled line-ahead, that is to say they sailed into the wind as much as possible. Once battle had been fully joined an offensive action might develop in three different ways: by massing against the enemy, aiming to achieve superiority at a decisive point, by enclosing the enemy between two lines of ships, one from the windward and the other from the leeward, or by breaking through the enemy's line. James Duke of York preferred formalism throughout when he fought, his intention being to meet the enemy van to van, centre to centre and rear to rear. Rupert, probably under the influence of Monck, sought to go into the attack in whichever way seemed most likely to be effective. In his last battle off the Texel what happened was that the French struggled to deal with the depleted Dutch van; Spragge and Tromp, who had a personal feud, concentrated on one another oblivious to everything else; while Rupert was left to fight de Ruyter's main force unaided by his other two squadrons. The result of this 'mêlée' fighting was unhappy. It might be compared with the Battles of Edgehill and Naseby on land: Rupert held his own on his own wing, but lost the battle. His temperament never really changed: it was '*toujours l'attaque*'.

After the signature of the Treaty of Westminster, which ended the Third Anglo–Dutch War in February 1674, Rupert's career as a commander came to a close. He was now fifty-four, a good age in the seventeenth century. But he still lived a full life. Before the war, in September 1668, he had been appointed constable of Windsor Castle and given apartments in the keep. John Evelyn in 1670 wrote as follows about a visit which he paid to them: 'Prince Rupert [as] Constable had begun to trim

up the keep or high round tower and handsomely adorned his hall with the furniture of arms which was very singular . . . from the hall we went into his bedchamber and ample rooms which were hung with tapestry, curious and effeminate pictures, as extremely different from the other, which presented nothing but war and horror, as was very surprising and diverting.' Besides being constable he was appointed lord lieutenant of Berkshire and Surrey. He was a founder member of the Hudson's Bay Company, which received its charter in 1670, and became its governor. Two Frenchmen had urged upon Charles II the importance of securing the bay, which opened up a new route to reach the valuable furs of Canada. It proved a profitable investment for the shareholders; the surrounding area was named Prince Rupert's Land in his honour. Rupert also became a member of the Council of Trade and Plantations. Originally there had been two advisory bodies consisting of

Rupert's participation in the Hudson's Bay Company, of which he was governor, resulted in the naming of adjacent lands in his honour, as this map shows.

185

paid experts who met twice a week but in September 1672 they were amalgamated. The Earl of Shaftesbury became president of the new body, John Locke the philosopher was soon to be appointed secretary, and various unpaid members, including Rupert, were added to it. He continued his association with the Royal African Company. Finally, he moved in the intellectual circles of his day, was a fellow of the Royal Society, and spent much time in his laboratories.

Through his association with Shaftesbury in the Hudson's Bay Company and the Council of Trade and Plantations he struck up a friendship with the future leader of the Whig party. According to a contemporary letter they were 'observed to converse very much together and are very great, and indeed I see his Highness's coach often at his [Shaftesbury's] door. They are looked upon as great Parliament men and for the interest of Old England . . .'

Shaftesbury's attitude to the government of Charles II became so critical that he was dismissed in the summer of 1679 from the post of Lord President of the Council. The name of Whig was given to those politicians who in the course of 1679–80 petitioned the King to recall his third parliament, which had been adjourned in the autumn of 1679. Rupert was among a group of twenty peers who tried to persuade Charles that Parliament must meet again in January 1680. The King calmly told the deputation that he wished everyone kept as good care of the country as he did, and ignored their advice. The fact was that Charles was determined to scotch a movement initiated in the House of Commons to exclude his brother James Duke of York, as a confessed Roman Catholic, from succession to the throne. It must have been a rather bizarre situation, with Rupert living at least part of the time in the same house as Charles II, who regularly visited Windsor Castle, while the Prince was becoming identified with the burgeoning Whig party.

Though Rupert never married, he was a normal heterosexual. Many stories of his relations with women have survived, some of them untrue or exaggerated. His friendship with the daughter of the governor of Linz when he was a young prisoner there, his admiration for the Duchess of Richmond in beleaguered Oxford, and his penchant for the German girl who

Rupert's mistress Peg Hughes, the actress, was said to have 'brought down and greatly subdued his natural fierceness'.

became in effect his elder brother's wife are all reasonably well documented.

In the spring of 1668 he took two months' holiday in Tunbridge Wells and met a young actress named Margaret or Peg Hughes, reputed to be the first woman to play the part of Desdemona in *Othello*. According to Anthony Hamilton's memoirs of the life of the Count of Grammont (1662–4), 'the impertinent gypsy chose to be attacked in form...', but it is plain that she was genuinely fond of Rupert and Rupert of her. If Hamilton

187

is to be trusted, she 'brought down and greatly subdued his natural fierceness'. She appears to have been modest enough and devoted to the Prince. He set her up as his mistress in 1673 at a house near Hammersmith; she bore him a daughter, who was named Ruperta and inherited her father's property in England.

Two years before his meeting with Peg Hughes, Rupert had a son by Francesca Bard, Lady Bellamont, the daughter of a Cavalier who had fought for the King in the First Civil War. Rupert first met Francesca during 1662, and she was to claim that he had married her; but if he did it is not clear why he never acknowledged the marriage, for she was a lady, daughter of an Irish peer, and not an actress, which was considered a low-grade occupation. Could German etiquette have been so strict? Dudley Bard, their son, was sent to Eton College when Rupert lived at Windsor. Afterwards Rupert prepared him for a military career; he was to be killed fighting as a volunteer at the siege of Buda in 1686. His father had left him his German properties. Both Rupert's mistresses survived him; his two children, Dudley and Ruperta, used to visit their father at Windsor Castle in his later years.

Besides the apartments in Windsor Castle and his establishment at Hammersmith, Rupert had a town house in Spring Gardens near St James's Park. He was evidently reasonably well-to-do. It was in Spring Gardens that he died on 29 November 1681 in his sixty-third year. He had always suffered from the head wound he received in the southern Netherlands, but the cause of his death was said to have been pleurisy. The picture painted by some of his biographers of his being a lonely man out of touch with the world at the end of his life, and finding consolation in his laboratory or with his hunting dogs, has little real basis. He had his mistresses and illegitimate children, like other courtiers of the day; he attended meetings of the Royal Society as well as the various official committees to which he had been appointed. As governor of the Hudson's Bay Company and a member of the Royal African Company he had plenty of outside interests. But he enjoyed his life at Windsor the most (just as King Charles II did), for there he could relax, hunt and experiment.

Rupert appointed William Lord Craven as the executor of

A late portrait of Rupert by the
miniaturist Samuel Cooper.

his will and the guardian of his daughter. Although Craven was
eleven years older than Rupert and had indeed been an admirer
of Rupert's mother, 'the Queen of Hearts', Craven was to out-
live Rupert by several years: he died in 1697 at the age of
eighty-nine. Craven was the chief mourner at Rupert's funeral

189

(the Prince was buried in Henry VII's chapel in Westminster Abbey) as well as his executor. Rupert had left his children and the actress Peg Hughes (who returned to the stage) well provided for, and ensured that his numerous household and outdoor servants were adequately rewarded. Among the treasures that the Earl of Craven discovered was an iron chest containing 1,694 guineas and a 'great pearl necklace' which was purchased by Nell Gwyn for £4,520. His pension of £3,000 a year from the King also appears to have been regularly paid. Clearly Rupert was never an extravagant man and so was able to bequeath valuable assets.

In judging Rupert as a commander, one must not think in terms of his brash youth, though self-confidence is not infrequently an asset. He learned from his experiences and proved himself adaptable to many different kinds of warfare. On land his tactics were an advance upon those of Gustavus Adolphus and on sea he followed in the footsteps of George Monck, a shrewd operator against the Dutch. Rupert showed himself excellent at improvisation, for example in his siege of Lichfield and in preparing his ships for the crossing of the Atlantic. But above all – and this is sometimes overlooked – he was an extremely capable organizer. As the late Lord Wavell and other writers on generalship have stressed, supply is the essence of victory in war: though a commander-in-chief hardly needs to be his own quartermaster, he must at least ensure that his quartermasters know their business. Many examples of Rupert's ability in this sphere can be read into the accounts of his sailing trip across the world; even more in the way in which he rapidly constructed and provisioned a navy in 1648 and 1649. No wonder he was critical of the corrupt organization of the Navy Board in Charles II's reign.

As has already been pointed out, the notion that Rupert was a cruel and ruthless German mercenary has little substance. He was of course a disciplinarian, but he rarely punished his own men or his enemies with death in cold blood. On the contrary he pleaded for and spared the lives of officers who appeared derelict in their duties or were accused of cowardice in action, for he appreciated the pressures to which fighting men are subjected. That again was why he was resentful of the charge of being a coward himself at Bristol. While on the surface he was a tough character, whom men did not thoughtlessly gainsay, inwardly he was sensitive. No doubt he was fully aware of the disapprobation of his conduct as a commander in the field expressed by some of the courtiers around King Charles I and of his unpopularity with the Navy Board after he settled in England in 1661. That his sensitivity made him vulnerable to criticism was probably his principal weakness, so that at times he must have been unhappy as well as unlucky.

Rupert's passionate temper, to which there is much testimony, was not necessarily an important defect of character. Commanders need to be tough. If they are not they will be disobeyed. Of his great opponent, Oliver Cromwell, it was written by one who knew him intimately that 'his temper' was 'exceeding fiery' though 'the flame of it was kept down for the most part'. The same could have been observed about Rupert. He did not tolerate intrigue, corruption or inefficiency, and the fussiness and volatility of King Charles I irked him. He felt easier at the way he was treated by his cousin, Charles II, who was adept at choosing good servants and allowing them to get on with their jobs. For his part Rupert was not, like Charles II, flexible. He was proud and touchy. He had no sympathy with merry Cavaliers like George Digby and George Goring. He treated his profession with the utmost seriousness. Though he was understandably resentful when Charles I condemned him for the loss of Bristol and when Charles II, egged on by Hyde, implied that he embezzled the prizes captured by his makeshift fleet, he remained unflinchingly loyal to the Stuarts as well as to his own family. Whatever his shortcomings may have been and however great was his lack of success in some of the outstanding battles of his career, Rupert was an honest and a noble man.

ACKNOWLEDGEMENTS

The photographs and illustrations in this book are reproduced by kind permission of the following. Those on pages 25 and 88, by permission of the Controller of Her Britannic Majesty's Stationery Office; pages 4, 6, 8–9, 10, 15, 19, 22, 36, 37, 39, 52, 57, 61, 63, 76, 83, 103, 119, 135, 141 and 160, the Mansell Collection; pages 2–3, 90, 104, 126, 128–9, 145, 162–3, 174–5, 183 and 187, the Radio Times Hulton Picture Library; pages 49, 50–51, 79, 114, 131, 134, 157, 170–71 and 185, Trustees of the British Museum; pages 20, 24, 26, 27, 31 and 94–5, National Army Museum; pages 166–7, 180–81 and 189, National Maritime Museum; pages 5, 68, 69 and 124, National Portrait Gallery; pages 87, 107 and 108, by John Freeman and Co.; pages ii, 109 and 146, by courtesy of the Earl of Dartmouth; page 41, by courtesy of the Publishers, Roundwood Press Ltd, Kineton, Warwick; page 85, Victoria and Albert Museum; page 101, by courtesy of Lord Saye and Sele; page 158, Ashmolean Museum, Oxford; page 172, Mary Evans Picture Library; page 146, from a private collection; and on page 69, the Collection of the Earl of Essex. Diana Phillips supplied the pictures. The maps were drawn by Bucken Limited.

SELECT
BIBLIOGRAPHY

Rupert's correspondence acquired from a descendant of one of
his secretaries is in Additional Mss 18980–2 in the British
Museum. Transcripts of most of these letters made for Sir
Charles Firth are in Firth Transcripts vols 6 to 8 bequeathed
by him to the Bodleian Library in Oxford. These transcripts
contain some additional material such as Captain Fearnes's de-
scription of the sinking of the *Constant Reformation* and a note
on Rupert's pensions. Prince Rupert's 'journal in England' was
printed by Firth in the *English Historical Review* for 1898.
Rupert's earliest biography dealing with his youth only is in
Lansdowne Mss 817 in the British Museum. Rupert's 'diary'
and 'logbook' are in the Wiltshire county archives at Trowbridge. Eliot Warburton, *Memoirs of Prince Rupert and the
Cavaliers* (3 vols, 1849) contains much of the material listed
above as well as a catalogue of the letters in Rupert's correspondence in the British Museum which he does not print. Warburton's transcripts are not entirely accurate, though the work of
this early Victorian historian has always been a treasure trove
for Rupert's numerous popular biographers. Other letters of
Rupert's are to be found in the Historical Manuscripts
Commission's report on the Dartmouth papers and in its ninth
report dealing with the Alfred Morrison collection. Some of his
letters are in George Bromley, *Collection of Original Royal Letters*
(1787) – Bromley was a descendant of Rupert – and in the
Pythouse Papers (ed W. A. Day, 1879).

Until recently there has been no good complete modern life
of Rupert – except for a short summary by Bernard Fergusson
entitled *Rupert of the Rhine* (1952). My friend Patrick Morrah has
been working on one for several years and kindly allowed me

to read it in manuscript. In it he makes excellent use of newly discovered sources, including the material at Trowbridge, which was not even known to the great Samuel Rawson Gardiner nor to Dame Veronica Wedgwood when they published their general histories of the English Civil Wars.

The best of the earlier biographies is Eva Scott's *Rupert: the Prince Palatine* (1899). She made use of the Firth transcripts as well as the material in the British Museum and original correspondence in the Bodleian, such as the Carte papers, but is weak on Rupert as a military commander.

Of the many popular lives of Rupert, George Edinger's *Rupert of the Rhine* (1936) is sprightly, but contains factual errors. He puts up a spirited argument (based on Warburton) for Rupert as the inventor of mezzotint, which I find convincing.

For the military background various books by Peter Young such as *Edgehill 1642* (1967) and *Marston Moor 1644* (1970) are invaluable. There is as yet no book on the royalist army comparable with Sir Charles Firth's book on *Cromwell's Army* (paperback 1962), but Dr Ian Roy is writing one.

For naval history the articles by R. C. Anderson on 'The Royalists at Sea' in *Mariner's Mirror* IX, XIV, XVII and XXI are essential. Michael Lewis, *The Navy of Britain* (1948) and *The History of the British Navy* (1959) are valuable introductions to a not very easy subject. For Rupert's voyage to the West Indies and back an excellent account is given by Richard Ollard, *Man of War* (1969). For the campaigns in Charles II's reign see *The Rupert and Monck Letter Book* (ed J. R. Powell and E. K. Timings, 1969), *Journals and Narratives of the Third Dutch War* (ed R. C. Anderson, 1946) and H. T. Colenbrander, *Bescheiden uit vreemde archieven omtrent de groote Nederlandsche Zeeoorlogen 1652–1676* (1919).

For a short book on the Civil War and an even shorter one on Rupert's famous foe, Oliver Cromwell, perhaps I may refer to two recent books of my own: *Oliver Cromwell and his World* (1972) and *A Concise History of the English Civil War* (1975).

INDEX